WALKING
EACH OTHER
HOME

**INTIMATE CONVERSATIONS ON WRITING AND
LIFE BY NOTABLE POETS OF THE 20TH CENTURY.**

I0532754

MICHAEL HOGAN

USA Publisher Cataloguing-In-Publication Data
Name: Hogan, Michael, 1943
Title: Walking Each Other Home: Intimate conversations on writing and life by notable poets of the 20th century. Michael Hogan.
Description: Laredo, Texas: Sinn Fein Editions, 2024. Interest age level 14 and up.
Identifiers: ISBN: 979-8-218-52477-7 (USA paperback).
Library of Congress Control Number: 2024921201

Subjects: Memoir, Creative writing, Poetry, American Literature, Irish Literature, Interviews and reflections with Edward Abbey (1927-1989), Agha Shahid Ali (1949-2001, Ai Ogawa (aka Florence Anthony (1947-2010)), Jon Anderson (1940-2007), Jimmy Santiago Baca (1952-), Ray Bradbury (1920-2012), Josephy Brodsky (1940-1996), Joesph Bruchac (1942-), Charles Bukowski (1920-1994), Tess Gallagher (1943-), Allen Ginsberg (1926-1997), Sam Hamill (1943-2018), Jane Hirshfield (1953-), Tony Hoagland (1953-2018), Richard Hugo (1923-1982), Galway Kinnell (1927-2014), Etheridge Knight (1931-1991), Gerald Locklin (1941-2021),W.S. Merwin (1927-2019), Czeslaw Milosz (1911-2004), Naomi Shihab Nye (1952-), Steve Orlen (1942-2016), Marge Piercy (1936-), Jaime Sabines (1926-1999), Reg Saner (1928-2021), Teo Savory (1907-1989), Richard Shelton (1933-2022), William Stafford (1914-1993), Thomas Valle (1947-2020).

Cover design by Ksenija Petranovic. Author photo by Lucinda Mayo. Earlier versions of some of these chapters first appeared as essays in the following publications: "Kissed by Allen Ginsberg" in *New Millennium Writings 2023* (recipient of the New Millennium Non-fiction Award); "From Prison to Yale: Jimmy Santiago Baca, *North American Project,* Winter, 2020, also in *Mexicans and Mexican Americans* (Guadalajara: Intercambio, 2023; "In the Time of the Jacarandas" in *Bravados: An Anthology*, ed Joyce Kimball (Lake Chapala: n/p).

The author is grateful to the University of Arizona Poetry Center, The Colorado Humanities Program, the San Francisco Education Fund, the Alden B. Dow Center for Creativity, the Irish Embassy in Mexico, and the Mexican Embassy in Ireland for their support and encouragement.

For Robert DiYanni

Author, editor, educator, and friend, with deep gratitude for his passion for literature, his love of learning, and his transformative mission demonstrating what teaching from the heart looks like.

"Who but me remembers? It's all melting away ... like snow ... a whole lifetime."

May Sarton

"The world is…a kind of spiritual kindergarten, where millions of bewildered infants are trying to spell God with the wrong blocks."

Edward Arlington Robinson

"When the moon rises too early to be of any use
I remember how old I am
and that I no longer have the option of dying young."

Richard Shelton

TABLE OF CONTENTS

FOREWORD

Once in a great while a book comes along that seizes your attention and sweeps you along in surprise and delight. Such a book you are about to read: Michael Hogan's splendid excursion into the world of poetry via his acquaintance and friendship with a host of contemporary poets. Michael Hogan takes us on a fascinating journey through conversations with these poets, excerpts from their poetry, and considerations about what poetry can mean and be and do for us throughout our lives.

Hogan's book vibrates with life, intimately linking thought with feeling. His book is a love song to life and literature and language—to teaching and learning, and to the people Hogan encounters in his devotion to the art of poetry and the craft of teaching. *Walking Each Other Home* demonstrates repeatedly what devotion looks like and sounds like in action—in the voices and visions of the poets Hogan interviews, shares conference presentation time with, and breaks bread with. Through lively conversations with his fellow poets, Hogan shows us what a true vocation can be—and why a calling that combines reading, writing, and teaching poetry matters deeply.

The book has a propulsive quality, as Hogan artfully blends dialogue and description with analysis and explanation to convey important truths about who we are and how and why our lives matter. And this, regardless of our beliefs and hopes about what may follow our allotted earthly span of life.

In reading *Walking Each Other Home*, you will experience surprises and discoveries, while overhearing Michael Hogan's conversations with poets, and reading his reflections on poetry as craft and art and experience. You will better understand how poetry offers us hope and consolation, how it helps us live our lives more fully, authentically, rewardingly.

Michael Hogan also provides tips for writing poetry and for reading it—guidance from the poets gathered here, Hogan's own advice mingled with theirs. This is just one of the many benefits you will derive from this engaging book.

As my NYU colleague Keith Meatto notes, Michael Hogan's book provides three key "P"s: *poetry, process,* and *pedagogy.* We are given poems in whole and part to savor; we are brought into the process of how poets make their poems; and we receive the gift of Michael Hogan's pedagogy—his expertise teaching the poems that permeate his pages, including, thankfully, some of his own.

Walking Each Other Home is a book to delight in, to treasure, to cherish. I look forward to sharing it with colleagues and friends. And I relish the opportunity to savor often both its pleasures and its wisdom.

Robert DiYanni
New York University

INTRODUCTION

"Poetry makes nothing happen," W. H. Auden wrote. Yet, as you will see in these pages, writers as diverse as a Russian émigré, an ex-convict, and a combat Marine, assure us convincingly that poetry saved their lives. This book is both an attempt to reconcile those seemingly contradictory statements as well as to provide texture to the lives of Nobel Prize laureate, Joseph Brodsky; former inmate, Etheridge Knight, and antiwar activist, Sam Hamill, along with seventeen others with whom I have studied, shared a stage with, or befriended.

Dylan Thomas wrote that "the force which through the green fuse drives the flower, drives my green life." To me, that line provides the reconciliation of the two conflicting views of poetry. By itself, the poem makes nothing happen. If readers don't interact with it, their inner lives proceed as before with no change, no new awareness. But given a reader who is alert and receptive, a good poem can often awaken an inner self that was asleep and now has discovered a new way of seeing. The "force," to steal Thomas's metaphor—through "the green fuse" of poetry –changes those of us who make ourselves available to it, and we have a new way of seeing. And when we change the way we look at things, the things we look at change.

I have seen it happen again and again as I shared poetry in detention centers, recovery homes, maximum security prisons, and with at-risk students in inner-city schools. I have also seen it occur, less dramatically but no less surely, in college classes and MFA writing workshops. It has also been my great good fortune to have had mentors along the way who have tossed out the lines of rescue to me, not once but twice in a lifetime, to pull me from a morass of self-destructive futility to a life of purpose and service. Poetry quite literally gave me a new life, built upon the wreckage of the old, but still my life, the ruins of the past forming a ballast in a sea of change.

This book is a miscellany of conversations I have had over the past forty years with powerful voices, some well-known, others less so, whose work provided a green fuse that, with the least spark of attention, will continue to ignite attentive readers today. At least half of those authors have died since I first began taking these notes, so the elegiac impulse is an additional motivator for memorializing their lives so that future generations can experience their vital presence as well as their poetry.

Although I use quotation marks in the dialogue sections, these are recreations of exchanges based on notes, journal entries, and my imperfect memory. As W.S. Merwin said of his many translations, they are "versions," and thus do not always fully render the speech patterns or nuances of the originals. But I believe they do render faithfully both the substance and the passion of the authors' remarks as I recall them.

Writers highlighted here began as *readers* of poetry who became so impressed with the "quietness and beauty" certain images brought to their minds, that they embarked on a long apprenticeship to attain mastery of the art. Some went far beyond that mastery and became known worldwide, receiving prizes and awards. Almost all became service providers of one sort or another, sharing their vision and words with public audiences, teaching their craft at universities and schools, or translating the work of fellow poets little known outside their own countries.

If one reads the biographical notes of poets, whether online, or on the back covers of their book, one usually sees the list of works they have published and the many honors and awards they have received. This is tiresome to many readers, who see the practice as a kind of boasting. But it is more an aspect of livelihood, a necessary horn tooting when one practices an art in a world that does not usually value the contemporary. Poetry books that sell in the thousands are usually those of dead poets such as Shakespeare, Whitman, or Frost. Just as paintings that sell for millions are invariably those by dead artists. Many poets live precariously from readings, guest lectures, grants, and awards. Others from teaching, and the universities often base promotion and salaries on a professor's publications. So, I have included a short bio note for each poet in deference to this need. But I hope readers will find more than sufficient reason to delve into their work beyond this flaunting, and appreciate the beauty and depth, not only of their work, but of their character and their contributions to our lives.

One will note that male poets here outnumber their female contemporaries. That is not by choice. Between the years 1974 and 1988 when I was studying, teaching, and performing in the United States, there were no women poets in residence at the University of Arizona nor at other western colleges or schools where I taught. I was blessed with two wonderful women professors who taught literature and short fiction (Susan Aiken and Francine Prose), but female poets were scarce on southwestern campuses in those days either as guest faculty or invited readers. Regrettably, of the fourteen recipients of the Pulitzer Prize for Poetry during those years, only three were women.

Many of the conversations here focus on craft, a major concern of mine and a topic to which all the writers responded enthusiastically with observations, tips, and strategies they utilized in their own work. But sometimes the conversations became more intimate, and we talked about life and discussed strategies to live more deeply and more meaningfully, and how poetry might help with that. For me, that is a precious gift, and one for which I am forever grateful. As William Carlos Williams once wrote, "You can't get the news from poetry, but people die every day from lack of what's found there."

CHAPTER ONE

YELLOW FLOWERS WITH RICHARD SHELTON

Richard Shelton (1933-2022) was a poet and English professor, author of nine books of poetry and several works of nonfiction. His memoir Going Back to Bisbee *was a* New York Times *Notable Book. He is equally renowned for his teaching at the University of Arizona, where he and his wife headed the Poetry Center for many years, and for his volunteer work in community and correctional settings. His former pupils include singer-songwriter Linda Ronstadt, poets Mark Doty and Jimmy Santiago Baca, and nature writer Ken Lamberton.*

I first met Richard Shelton at a low point in my life. My father had just died, and I was at loose ends. At the suggestion of a dear friend and fellow writer, Susan North, I joined a community workshop that Shelton had organized in Florence, Arizona. I had read some of his work and I felt that he was a poet who had genuine insights into tragedy, loss, and the pain of isolation that I could relate to. Reading some of his poems was like pressing my tongue on an aching tooth. It made the ache all the more painful but was somehow a relief. I didn't realize then that the workshop would be transformative, or that Shelton would enable me to do what he had done, and translate the pain of ordinary life into art. I didn't know then that I would form a lifetime friendship with one of the noblest human beings I have ever known, and that this friendship would enable me to reach a new depth in my own poetry and to live a much richer life.

The poet Mark Doty, who met Shelton when he was in high school, credits Shelton with revealing to him his vocation as a writer. Doty had spent most of his childhood and adolescence moving around the country, following a father who worked with the Army Corps of Engineers. In Tucson, one of his teachers introduced him to Shelton, who read his early poems and provided encouragement. Doty recalls being invited, in the Sixties, to Shelton's home where his wife Lois was playing the piano and singing pieces from the *ThreePenny Opera* in their book-lined living room. Doty recalls, "I felt a window had opened in another world. He showed me that one could have a life where art and literature could be central to one's experience."

My own experience was equally illuminating. Listening to Shelton interacting with other workshop participants, I saw how one could be modest yet assertive. How one could teach without preaching, instruct without commanding.

The workshop was open to all comers. Some of the poems read were dreadful: antiquated word choices with *thee* and *thou* predominating, meter-less rhyme; others were gushy, overly sentimental. Still others were raging against fate while themselves playing havoc with sense and sound.

No matter how absurd or poorly written the piece, Shelton always had something encouraging to say or he was able to suggest that the person read a poet who might give them some insight into how to handle the subject of their own poem more skillfully. He always remembered to bring, either in book form or photocopies, the poems he prescribed and give them to the participants to read aloud. Not everyone profited, of course, but a few did. And even those whose work did not significantly improve were able to read other writers with pleasure and from these several contemporary poets suddenly had new fans. As with most writing workshops, there was often a talented member or two whom we all recognized, and I was privileged to be among that number.

It resulted in after-class meetings and suggestions for revision and publication, which I took advantage of. I date my earliest and some of my best publications from the advice and suggestions of Shelton which included *New Letters*, *The Harvard Review*, *The American Poetry Review*, and the *Paris Review*. In addition, I applied, at his suggestion, for a fellowship from the National Endowment for the Arts. With his encouragement I went on to receive an MFA in Creative Writing (also with a fellowship stipend) from the University of Arizona and spent more than thirty fruitful years in a teaching career abroad.

More importantly, I learned how to integrate the death of my father and later the more terrible loss of my young son into my teaching and found that both losses made me a more compassionate, more open person, rather than one closed off and made bitter by pain and despair. During the many hours we spent together, I recorded a few of Shelton's aphorisms; many of which I consulted with profit during my teaching career.

- *Your students don't care what you know, Michael, unless they know that you care. Show them by your conversations and example that you care for each of them, and you will come to love the job and be loved.*

- *I don't usually tell people I'm a poet when they ask. It seems to me to be presumptuous and a bit absurd. I say simply, I am a teacher.*

- *I know that many events in your life will seem momentous, but the most momentous is the heating up of our planet. Find ways to warn the world of this and ways to implement low energy and low consumption of resources in your daily life. This is your obligation to the next generation.*

- *Don't go about with a sad face regretting the mistakes you've made. Try to see what you learned from them and find ways of sharing that with others who are in doubt or despair. Never preach. Share.*

- *Success is sometimes nothing more than what we do with the mess we've made of our lives.*

- *Read, read, read! As Aldous Huxley once wrote: "There is no great writing without great reading."*

- *Imitate other poets from time to time until your own voice comes back to you.*

- *Read widely, especially outside of literature. Read history, physics, philosophy, political science, and economics. Learn the vocabularies of other disciplines; they will enrich your own.*

- *It's okay to talk behind someone's back as long as you are speaking well of them. If you want to criticize, check yourself. Most criticism is self-righteous and self-aggrandizing. It is seldom helpful when done face to face and never when done out of their presence.*

- *Sarcasm, especially with students, is a kind of bullying. Try to avoid it even though it can be tempting. It can cause pain and leave scars.*

For over forty years, Dick Shelton and I have been friends. He literally changed my life and suggested new ways of seeing the world. I remember one class in which I wrote a poem that I thought was particularly wonderful. It was about the fluorescence of the Sonoran Desert after the August monsoon when the desert becomes transformed with carpets of yellow blossoms. I wrote in my poem:

> *A sea of yellow flowers flowing over the Sonoran hills*
> *on a sun-capped inland tide all the way to Mexico.*

The poem was melodious and original. It was rooted in the local, the concrete. It had both sound and sense, metaphor and movement. I thought it was wonderful. When I finished reading, Shelton, who could be gentle with those who were weak but merciless to his chosen few, stared at me for a moment. *What kind of yellow flowers, Michael?*

"What do you mean," I spluttered. "What kind? Just yellow flowers."

"There are over twenty varieties of yellow flowers in the Sonoran Desert. Don't you think that if you live here and write about the land you should know the names of a few? Or are you not that serious as a poet?

"What do you suggest?" I asked, annoyed.

Shelton smiled away my anger and said in a quiet voice, "We offer a course in Biology here at the University called *Flora and Fauna of the Southwest*. I suggest you sign up for it next semester."

I did, and several others in the class did as well. I was not alone in the narrowness of my humanities education.

The course turned out to be more interesting than I expected. Not only did I learn the names and uses of hundreds of plants, but the field trips over several weeks took our group through five different life zones. From the extended stretch of desert floor with the Giant Saguaros, golden poppies and creosote, to the scrub oaks of Zone Two with its spindly pines, otherworldly *palo verde*, and the pale lilac of *verbena*. Then Zone Three, a ponderosa pine forest with the rich odor of coniferous trees growing more and more vigorous as we ascended.

After a rather cool evening campout and a morning spent classifying drawing, and cataloging samples from the previous days we hiked up to Zone Four, where we found fir trees and hemlock, even spruce and cypress as in the Colorado and Canadian forests. Along the way were Canadian maples sharing their fall colors in the autumn sun and all along the creek aspens flashed their silver dollars in the mist that rose from the water. Finally, at the top, a lush meadow and then a short hike to where a light snowfall had partially covered the summit where we rested and looked out over the forest and desert and distant city below. It was a transcendent moment there on the top of Mount Lemmon. Richard Shelton had given me a gift that would last a lifetime.

Much later, when I told Dick Shelton that he had changed my life many years before, he said that I was prone to romantic notions and hyperbole. "Not in this case," I said. When he asked for an example of this change, I said, "the yellow flowers class." He looked at me skeptically. "What?"

"It's a long story," I said, knowing that there are some things that even great mentors cannot guess at.

CHAPTER TWO

LEARNING TO PRAISE WITH MARGE PIERCY

Marge Piercy (b. 1936-) is the author of several novels, short stories, and volumes of poetry. She is a socialist, feminist, and an anti-war activist. She has received numerous literary awards. Her prose includes historical novels and science fiction. In poetry she tends to focus on social issues, including income disparity, but she has also been lauded for her lyricism in praise of the ordinary life.

During my childhood in the Fifties (before television, computers and the ubiquitous iPhone), my parents and my sister used to read to each other in the evenings. Following Bishop Fulton Sheehan's advice, "the family that prays together, stays together," we told our beads and said a decade of the rosary. Then my mother would read a poem or two from *A Treasury of Poetry*, a heavy doorstop of a volume bound in Kelly green cloth that indiscriminately contained both good poetry and bad. As we got older, we would pass the book around and choose one of our favorites.

Among the women poets was Emily Dickinson, of course, and my favorite of hers was the Civil War poem "Success is counted

Sweetest/By those who ne'er succeed." My sister enjoyed Elizabeth Barret Browning's sonnets from the Portuguese, especially "How do I love thee, let me count the ways." My Dad appreciated Marianne Moore, who was once hired by Ford to name a new car. He loved how she wrote that poetry is for those who prefer "imaginary gardens with real toads in them." And we all enjoyed "Recuerdo" by Edna St. Vincent Millay. "We were very tired, we were very merry/We had gone back and forth all night on the ferry." My mother, who preferred a woman in a dramatic situation, rather than as author, enjoyed reciting "Barbara Frietchie" by John Greenleaf Whittier. The poem depicts an elderly Yankee woman in Virginia during the height of the Civil War who flies the Stars and Stripes from her balcony as the Confederate cavalry passes her home. When a rebel soldier takes aim at her, she shouts out defiantly from her bedroom window. "*Shoot if you must this old gray head/But spare your country's flag.*" The chivalric Southern general in charge then orders the trooper to leave her unmolested.

Although I took a survey course in modern literature at Stonehill College (1961-3) and later studied poetry at Boston College and Boston University (1963-64), in those days, there were few poems by women that we looked at. I remember several, of course, by Elizabeth Barrett Browning and Emily Dickinson, and a couple by Elizabeth Bishop but little else. The late Sixties and early Seventies changed all that. There was an explosion of writing by women and a new vehicle on the block: the small press literary magazine, funded by small grants from the National Endowment for the Arts (thanks to Lyndon Johnson). One could hardly pick up a magazine without encountering several poems by talented women, among them, Denise Levertov, Sylvia Plath, Adrianne Rich, and Sonia Sanchez.

By the mid-Seventies I was on another university campus, this time on a graduate fellowship in the University of Arizona writing program in Tucson. With the advice of Susan North, a Tucson poet, I read more widely, including the work of Jane Hirshfield, Sharon Olds, Maya Angelou, and Mary Oliver. I enrolled in Professor Susan Aiken's course "Women Writers of the 20th Century" and was exposed to Lucille Clifton, Margaret Atwood, Naomi Shihab Nye, and a host of others.

I consumed poems from these and other authors with relish and often wrote reviews in several literary magazines. Soon I was getting packages of new books from publishers and requests from magazine editors from authors to write reviews of work by these and other poets. I was even approached by Bill Henderson, founder of the Pushcart Press to be guest editor for the famous Pushcart Prize. Now reading hundreds of magazines and chapbooks, I was quite overwhelmed. I was spending so much time on these activities that I had missed the date for a critical paper due for Professor Susan Aiken's class and had to take an "incomplete" or risk my fellowship.

Now with free time, since I had no major paper due, I was looking for a bit of part time work to augment my meager fellowship. Fortunately, an angel appeared in the form of Marge Piercy, a poet in Wellfleet, Massachusetts. I had written reviews of two of her books, *To Be of Use*, and *Living in the Open*. She wondered if I would be interested in editing her newest book, *The Twelve Spoked Wheel*, and helping her select the strongest poems. Not only was I flattered and willing to do so, but she also offered me a consulting fee which would pay a month's expenses. Her past work had excited me, and I was anxious not only to read the new poems but also to have an exchange of ideas with her.

Piercy had achieved a mastery of the concise image in her poems, which often surprised the reader with a leap of sudden awareness. I am reminded of what Dickinson said about how she recognized a good poem. "If I read a book and it makes my whole body so cold no fire can warm me I know that is poetry. If I feel physically as if the top of my head were taken off, I know that is poetry. These are the only ways I know it. Is there any other way?" In Piercy's disturbing "Rape Poem," she writes

> *There is no difference between being raped*
> *And being pushed down a flight of cement steps*
> *Except that the wounds also bleed inside.*

And the fear of rape is pervasive, especially for the woman living alone.

> *Never to open the door to a knock*
> *Without that razor just grazing the throat.*
> *The fear of the dark side of the hedges,*
> *The back seat of the car, the empty house*
> *Rattling keys like a snake's warning....*

As my mother would say, Piercy doesn't mince words. She is brutally explicit. Many of her so-called "feminist poems" such as this one, I believe, are really addressed to men in the hope that they might see more clearly.

In the ironic "To the Pay Toilet" she reminds us of the failure of our capitalist system:

Most blatantly you shout that waste of resources
for the greatest good of the smallest number
where twenty pay toilets line up glinty clean
and at the end of the row one free toilet
oozes from under its crooked door,
while a row of weary women carrying packages and babies
wait and wait and wait to do
what only the dead find unnecessary...

But besides the telling and brutal image she is also capable of surprising grace and beauty. As in the poem "We Become New" which describes the act of falling in love.

When I am turning slowly
in the woven hammocks of our talk,
when I am chocolate melting into you,
I taste everything new
in your mouth.

When I mentioned to her that I had shared this last poem with students and that one boy had reported that he, in turn, read it to his girlfriend, she responded in a lovely letter. She reminded me that kind of sharing is what Emily Dickinson embraced when she dropped off poems among neighbors, and what Sam Hammill called the "gift economy." But she said that she preferred to think about the conservation of energy. The words below are paraphrased from that letter. To my best recollection, she explained it this way:

"We know from physics that energy cannot be created or destroyed. It is the E of Einstein's $E=mc2$. So, the inspiration of the poem and its images is pure mental and emotional energy which becomes matter when it is inscribed on the page. Then it becomes energy again when the reader inhabits it. Then it becomes matter again when the reader shares it with another or copies it down. Then energy again when the next person hears it or picks it up and reads it. And on and on.

"Some writers wonder whether their name or their work will outlast them. Whether it will become part of the canon. But that does not concern me. I know that once a poem is out there and read by two or three people, its life goes on and will go on long after I am no longer here. I have no control over that, nor do I want any. Although I do admit it delights me when I hear reports such as yours of one of my poems out there living a full life!"

I remarked that some of her poems touched on pain, tragedy, mortality, the abuse and humiliations suffered by the poor and disenfranchised, the anger felt by women excluded from a system controlled by a patriarchal hierarchy or born into an abusive family. And I asked if this didn't depress rather than inspire the poetic impulse. She had been accused by some reviewers of didacticism and argumentation in some of her feminist poems, and I inquired how she would respond.

She answered that she seldom responded to negative criticism, especially if it did not propose a remedy. And that she felt the impulse to righteous anger at injustice, a refusal to accept a demeaning status quo, and a pride that rejected humiliation, was positive. It comprised the virtues of courage, integrity and grit. The characteristics of a woman warrior. And in that sense, each poem was a poem of praise. Not praising the world as it is, but the woman as she is, and the world as it could be.

Marge and I would connect in person in 1989 when we were both invited to give readings out in San Francisco. Shortly thereafter, I went to Mexico, and we lost touch. It was not until the invention of Facebook that we connected again: she in Wellfleet, I in Guadalajara. In 2022 in failing health at the age of 86, she suffered from heart trouble and glaucoma and wrote about her difficulties. I was reading Schopenhauer's *Maxims and Reflections* at the time and quoted that pessimistic philosopher in a FB message to her. *As we age, we discover that happiness is simply the absence of pain.*

Marge was not happy with that. For her the glass would always be half full. She wrote back, "Since I already died, these days I enjoy whatever I can. Even the sight of a tree moves me and makes me happy. Woody [Ira Woods, her husband], my cats, my home, reading—all a joy!"

I remembered then a breakfast conversation with W S. Merwin about the first tree of our childhoods. And I remembered too, his suggestion that I read more Rilke. I picked up the book that I knew

Marge loved as well and that influenced her world view. In his *Letters on Life*, Rilke wrote:

> *And so it is that most people have no idea how beautiful the world is and how much magnificence is revealed in the tiniest things, in some flower, in a stone, in tree bark, or in a birch leaf. The grown-ups, going about their business and worries, and tormenting themselves with all kinds of details, gradually lose the perspective for these riches that children, when they are attentive and good, soon notice and love with their whole heart.*

Thank you, Marge Piercy, for that timely reminder and for bringing me back to that clear simplicity.

A BRILLIANT AND SAVORY FIRST BOOK.

Teo Savory (1907-1989) was a novelist, poet, translator, and publisher. Born in Hong Kong, her family moved to the US in 1915. She attended the Royal College of Music in London and began writing musical comedy. She also wrote six widely praised novels, three collections of short stories and four books of poems. In 1958 she married the poet, translator, and book designer, Allan Brilliant and together they founded Unicorn Press in 1966.

Teo Savory had edited and published several books in the Sixties and Seventies including meditations by Thomas Merton, poetry by Robert Bly, Kenneth Rexroth, and John Haines. She and her husband, Alan Brilliant, also translated and published poems by Gunter Eich, Garcia Lorca, Eugéne Guilleric, Tristan Corbiere, and other major European writers. I had read and reviewed some of these which were beautifully designed and handsomely printed on letterpress.

Although, at the time, I had only published occasional poems and articles in small magazines, I decided to send a sizable group of poems to Teo back in the early Seventies. She graciously responded by commenting on a few of the poems and writing "If the whole MS were as good as these three or four, we would eagerly publish. Not quite there yet. Please query us again when it is."

The finalized manuscript, *Letters for My Son,* was published in 1975 with an encouraging back cover blurb from the poet William Stafford, followed by brisk sales which resulted in multiple reprints. What was even more interesting, however, was the correspondence we had in the intervening months about the press, and the editors' friendships with some of the movers and shakers of the Forties and Fifties. Most notable of these was Alger Hiss.

Teo had previously worked in New York as an executive and publicist for New York's American National Theater and the Woodstock Playhouse and established an agency that handled television scripts. She had been an active supporter of the New Deal and had befriended many Roosevelt officials in her day. Some of these she helped by editing their articles or proposals. She often used her connections to get them published. One editor she knew well was the infamous Whittaker Chambers, the editor at *Time* magazine. She was also friends with a sophisticated and brilliant Harvard Law School graduate previously mentioned, Alger Hiss.

When Chambers was accused of being a communist in the Fifties by the House Un-American Activities Committee (HUAC), he was asked to provide the names of other communists or communist sympathizers that he knew. Seeking to mitigate whatever penalties might be forthcoming, Chambers provided them with a long list, including Alger Hiss, one of the most respected members of the New

Deal. He embroidered this revelation by adding that Hiss, while working for the State Department, even provided him with secret documents.

It is important to remember that this occurred during a time of Red-baiting and Commie-hunting. Many who hated the New Deal reforms of FDR, had transferred this antipathy to Truman. They sought to undermine the hold the Democratic Party had on the voters since the 1932 elections. Among those who joined in the fray was a young Congressman by the name of Richard Nixon, followed in short order by Senator Joe McCarthy, both unknown at the time. One later rose to national prominence and the presidency, the other to a short-lived but senselessly destructive infamy.

The sacrificial lamb in the case was Alger Hiss, a well-known and well-placed liberal, he had served as law clerk to two Supreme Court justices, accompanied FDR to Yalta, worked on the Marshall Plan, and was the first secretary general of the United Nations. Now, as president of the Carnegie Endowment for International Peace, he was the perfect target. When summoned before the HUAC he did not plead the Fifth Amendment but protested his innocence. Chambers (protected from a defamation lawsuit by Congressional immunity) doubled down on his accusations. This time he produced documents he said were smuggled to him by Hiss in a pumpkin left on his farm. The documents were known as the Pumpkin Papers.

Defenders of Hiss, such as Secretary of State Dean Acheson declared that President Truman's opponents were making a sacrificial lamb out of Hiss. Truman himself declared that HUAC was using "red herrings" to defame Hiss. Acheson declared,

> *I will not turn my back on him...I think every person who has known Alger Hiss or has served with him at any time has upon his conscience the very serious task of deciding what his attitude is and what his conduct should be. That must be done by each person in the light of his own standards and his own principles.*

Ultimately Hiss was convicted of perjury after lying about whether he actually knew Chambers (he did but by a different name) and was sent to prison for 5 years. Released after 44 months, he was unable to find work. Teo Savory and her friends who had supported him through the ordeal were able to get him a job after his release in 1954, as a salesman for the stationery company, S. Novick & Sons, in New York City. In 1957, he published *In the Court of Public Opinion*, a book challenging in detail the prosecution's case against him.

In 1975 the Justice Department released copies of the Pumpkin Papers. One roll of film was totally blank due to overexposure, two others were faintly legible copies of non-classified Navy Department documents relating to such subjects as life rafts and fire extinguishers, and the remaining two were photographs of innocuous State Department memoranda.

A few days later, after examining the so-called "evidence", the Massachusetts Supreme Court stated in a unanimous decision that, despite his conviction, Hiss had demonstrated the "moral and intellectual fitness" required to be an attorney. Hiss was the first lawyer ever readmitted to the Massachusetts bar after a major criminal conviction. As for Nixon, it wouldn't be until the release of all the Nixon tapes that we got the real story. Nixon said on tape:

> *We won the Hiss case in the papers. We did. I had to leak stuff all over the place. Because the Justice Department would not prosecute it. Hoover didn't even cooperate.... It was won in the papers. I leaked out the papers.... I leaked out the testimony. I had Hiss convicted before he ever got to the grand jury.... It wasn't done waiting for the goddamn courts or the attorney general or the FBI.*

The Nixon Tapes (Touchstone, 1998), pp 338-339).

CHAPTER THREE

BREAKFAST WITH W. S. MERWIN

W.S. Merwin (1927-2019) was the 17th Poet Laureate of the United States. He wrote more than 50 books of poetry and prose and translated several others. He was the recipient of both the Pulitzer Prize and the National Book Award. A lifelong advocate of ecology and reforestation, he dedicated his time and his personal resources to those endeavors.

It was a cool March morning in Tucson back in 1977 when I rode my bicycle over to the Poetry Center at the University of Arizona. Adjacent to the Center's library and office building but separated by a tree-bordered and dapple-shaded lawn, was the Poetry Cottage where the visiting writer was housed. W.S. Merwin was the invited poet that week and, as part of his mandate, shared his work and observations on poetry to a small group of creative writing majors. Steve Orlen, the instructor, had passed around a signup sheet at the end of the session the previous day so that those of us who wished for a more personal touch could have a 20-minute interview with the poet to discuss our own work. I signed up for 8 am, gave Merwin a copy of my recent chapbook, told him how much I enjoyed his poetry, and that I looked forward to speaking with him in the morning.

When I arrived at 7:55 the following day, Merwin met me at the door dressed casually in tan slacks, a colorful Hawaiian shirt of blue and ochre floral design, brown leather sandals and a welcoming smile.

"Michael, so good to see you!"

Despite the casual attire, I had the overwhelming impression of a very formal man. His accent was eastern upper class, his posture erect, and his bearing gracious. There was a genuine warmth there as well. He had charisma in spades.

He offered me a seat at the dining room/kitchen table. He said that there were only two other signups for the private session that morning and that, if I didn't have anything planned, perhaps I would be interested in breakfast with him, and we could have a much longer chat. I readily agreed. He began by speaking about a piece in my chapbook, *Letters for My Son.*

"I especially liked your poem about the young boy under a welcoming maple tree thinking about the future and the places he would go, but then the poem ends with the line *on that summer day, which was all his lifetime.*" Very moving," Merwin said offhandedly.

I was both amazed and delighted that he not only read my chapbook but liked one of the pieces so much he remembered a line.

"I also had a tree in my backyard in New Jersey when I was a boy, "Merwin continued. "I used to speak to it, hold long conversations sometimes. I think Rilke says somewhere that the first tree of our childhood is all the trees of our life; it is from that one that we trace our love of them all. How do you like your eggs? Is scrambled okay?"

I assured him that scrambled was fine, as he poured me a glass of orange juice. I reached into my backpack and took out the two of his books that I brought to be inscribed.

"I have a couple of your books, Mr. Merwin...."

"Oh please, call me Bill."

"Well, Bill, I brought *The Lice,* and the *Miner's Pale Children.* I liked your poem about trees in *The Lice.* Well, maybe 'liked' is not the word. I mean it is about cutting down trees, so it was upsetting, moving, but also somehow satisfying because the destruction the woodcutters cause to the environment eventually comes to envelop them."

"Ah yes," he replied, serving the eggs. "And here is some excellent Sonoran salsa, *muy picante,* as they say in Mexico. Yes, the poem you mean is "The Last One." It is kind of a reverse creation myth. The developers cut down the trees, *because why not?* —a line which reflects the assumption that man is the master of the universe. He can cut down or destroy whatever he wishes. So, the poem is a destruction narrative with a karmic twist. Nothing is left in the end but shadows of the things they have cut down and eventually those shadows whisk the men away as well in the end. Nature will have her revenge. She will have the last word.

"I do not think it is possible, Michael, to be a poet who matters, if one is not in love with the natural world. It is what I detected in your work--this love. And of course, in Dick Shelton's poems as well whose passion for the Sonoran Desert inspires his work. You have chosen a good mentor there or did he choose you? No, don't answer that. It is rhetorical. Master and student find each other. It is magical and not to be examined too closely.

"So, about your work… It is quietly powerful. You have a good ear for the music of the syllables and the spaces between them. I can tell you read a great deal. If I had to guess at influences I would say, Dylan Thomas, maybe Robert Frost, perhaps William Stafford, and that you have read and absorbed all the classics. Good guesses? You have some mastery of the narrative poem and a sensitivity for the local, an eye for concrete particulars. However, there is a tendency to sometimes say too much, the early childhood influence of Tennyson and Longfellow, no doubt! So as an antidote, I would suggest reading more Dickinson and learn to say things on the slant occasionally, and in a more compressed fashion. I *know*, I should talk. I often wax prosaic as well. But that is why I published a book of prose pieces, *The Miner's Pale Children,* to allow that form to grow more on its own."

I had been taking notes and Merwin paused and smiled suddenly. "I'm sorry, Bill," I said. "I should have asked. Do you mind if I write some notes?"

"Not at all, Michael. I'm flattered that you find my pearls of wisdom useful. I am impressed that you came prepared with a pen and notebook. I am told by most teachers that it is rare these days.

"It reminds me of a story. Paul Auster, a fine writer and translator, talks about the time when he was a young boy of about eight years and his father took him to his first big league baseball game. The boy was a big fan of the New York Giants and Willie Mays was his hero. Anyway, the boy and his parents were invited by a couple who had box seats at Yankee Stadium, and it was quite a big deal.

"After the game, his parents sat talking with their friends while all the fans departed. When he and his family finally got up to leave, who appeared from the locker rooms but the famous Willie Mays, the boy's hero. He gathered his courage and approached the legend and asked him for his autograph.

"*Sure, kid,* Willie Mays, replied. *You got a pen?* The boy didn't have one. He asked his father. Nope, nor did any of the grownups. *Sorry kid, Willie, said. No pen, no autograph. Got to go!* From then on, Paul Auster always carried a pen with him, and from that summer day, when he was eight years old, he credits his vocation to becoming a writer. *If you have a pen with you all the time,* he would say, *you're quite likely to start using it.*

"So, Paul Auster. Did I mention that he was a translator? Besides writing novels, screenplays, essays and poetry, he also translated Stéphane Mallarmé, Philippe Petit, André Brouchet, and others. So, I think it is important that you read poetry from other countries. Certainly in translation, but also you should have one or two you can read in the original. Do you have any languages?"

"Four years of Latin, of course, from Christian Brothers, and then two years of French and two years of Spanish in college."

"Well, from Latin certainly the *Odes of Horace*. That is a must. Now in Spanish, Octavio Paz, Pablo Neruda, Jaime Sabines for starters. Then in French, am I going too fast? No? Well then, Baudelaire, Paul Eluard,

Jacques Prévert and Paul Valéry. That's a good start. I won't overburden you with much German, much more difficult than the Romance tongues but some Goethe at least in translation and all of Rilke but especially *Sonnets of Orpheus*."

"I have read some Rilke in translation."

"Ah, yes?"

"Letters to a Young Poet, of course, and some of the *Sonnets.*"

"Do you recall any?"

"One particular poem struck me that I can still recall. I believe it was *The Bust of Apollo.*"

"Ah, yes. I believe it is called 'The Archaic Torso of Apollo.' It has a famous last line.

Do you recall it?"

"For here there is no place that does not see you. You must change your life."

'Yes. What do you make of that line, Michael?'

"Well, it is a flat statement which is always risky in a poem. But it grabs me as a reader. It is also a *salto* as they say in Spanish, a leap in logic. How did he go from a headless body by an unknown sculptor to an authoritative imperative that includes the reader?"

"It is a line that will follow you, you know. It is like the drawing of a tree in which you are invited to find the women concealed in the branches. Once you see the image of the woman you can never unsee it. *You must change your life.*"

"But what exactly might that mean?" I asked. "What if readers think their life is fine just as it is?"

"Then, I suggest that they are not truly paying attention to the poem or to their lives. Note how Rilke first brings us to the bust of Apollo. It is merely a bust. No head, no limbs. Yet, it shines with an interior light. And from this minimalist representation we can infer the whole."

"Like a poem!"

"As you say, Michael. Like a poem, or like any work of art that is in the least masterful. Not because of the materials used, or MFA, or other degree of the maker, but because of an image or thought that was gifted, in which the maker somehow breathed in a spiritual connection."

"From which we get the word *inspired.* But maybe we are reading too much into the line here."

"Or not enough," quipped Merwin.

"What do you mean?"

"Well, you asked about the reader. He is not only addressing himself and what the art meant to him, but also the reader and what the art should suggest, not command, the viewer to do."

"But the reader…"

"*Hypocrite lecteur. mon semblable, mon frère,* wrote Baudelaire. The viewers who don't feel they need to change their lives are mistaken. They either do not have self-knowledge or they are being hypocritical. It means that they are not taking their life seriously. *Hypocrite lecteur.* But also, they are no different from the narrator (or the poet) who also fails from time to time. They are his likeness, his brother (*semblable, frère*) An artist or a poet should be working each day to develop their gift. To use one's talent to its fullest, as the parable from Matthew suggests. But often we are content to just show up now and then when inspired or settle for a first draft which is 'good enough' or rely on our reputation or previous work to be published or get an exhibition, then we fail ourselves and our gift."

"And what about people who are not poets or artists? How might it apply to them?"

"You tell me, Michael. I have done enough telling for today."

"Well, maybe when we catch a glimpse of beauty, even a shadow of it, we should try to emulate that in our own lives. That is to say, whatever task we have to perform throughout the day we should do so with care and with love.

"As in Salinger's *Franny and Zooey*. Do you know that book?

"Yes, where she says she is learning how to pray incessantly."

"Exactly, and what is that but a daily reminder to make heart and hand join together? To change your life is not a one-time affair but a daily challenge. And once you truly see that, Michael, it is like the image of the woman in the tree, you cannot unsee it. You must change your life. It is a lifetime's work and a joyful one. As the poet Jaime Sabines used to say, *Gracias a dios, tenemos chamba, nuestro regalo inolvidable.* Thank God we have work, our unforgettable gift. And that work is simply to be the best we can be with the brief life we have been given."

CHAPTER FOUR

LEARNING HUMILITY FROM GALWAY KINNELL

Galway Kinnell (1927-2014) was a Pulitzer Prize winning poet and social activist. During the Civil Rights Movement he worked to promote voter registration and was also active in protests during the Vietnam War. He was arrested several times for his efforts. A lifelong admirer of Walt Whitman, his poetry is grounded in reality rather than imagination.

I was fortunate during two of my years in Arizona to have the use of a house on Mabel Street in Tucson, a home owned by the writer Susan North who had a ranch just outside the city. My proximity to the University and my love for poetry led Lois Shelton, director of the Poetry Center to ask a favor. Would I mind hosting visiting poets coming through, taking them from the airport, feeding them and transporting them to the evening reading? I readily acquiesced. I was especially delighted with this task because I had custody of my thirteen-year-old son and thought the exposure to these talented writers would be educational. So, when I had the schedule of the writers who would be coming through, I began getting copies of their books and choosing selected poems which would be accessible to read with my son. Thus, when we picked up a poet at the airport, we both would have something to say about their work and make them feel welcome.

We met Galway Kinnell at Tucson International by the luggage carousel and carried his bags to my car. "So, how was your flight?" I asked.

"Terrible, he replied. "Lots of turbulence and poor in-flight service. It was chilly and I couldn't even get a blanket. That's the last time I'll fly with that airline!"

While I was loading the luggage, he got into the back seat of our family car, treating it as if it were a taxi, rather than riding in front with the host. It made conversation a bit strained, but I ventured a few remarks.

I shared a bit about the Poetry Center. I mentioned rather proudly some of the distinguished guests it had hosted over the years from Frost through Auden, and how honored we were to have him as a part of the Reading Series this year. His responses were monosyllabic grunts.

I knew he was a fan of Whitman, so I mentioned that sadly the Good Gray Poet had never been a guest reader and didn't even get the expected chuckle. But I am a persistent person, so I began reciting lines from the "Learn'd Astronomer" poem with the comment that despite Whitman's disparagement of such studies, I had signed up for an astronomy course in grad school. Perhaps you remember the lines:

When I heard the learn'd astronomer,

*When the proofs, the figures, were ranged in columns before
me,*

*When I was shown the charts and diagrams, to add, divide,
and measure them,*

*When I sitting heard the astronomer where he lectured with
much applause in the lecture-room,*

How soon unaccountable I became tired and sick,

Till rising and gliding out I wander'd off by myself,

Kennell finished the poem.

"In the mystical moist night-air, and from time to time,

Look'd up in perfect silence at the stars.

So, you would challenge that?" he asked. "Why?"

"Well," I said, "because the *mystical night air* in reality is far more interesting than just a poetic trope. It is a rich universe, and I think that the more I know about it, the deeper my life and my understanding will be, and perhaps my poetry as well."

"And the sense of wonder?"

"I think it will grow, not wither away."

"Humph," was Kinnell's response and he settled back into silence.

Then, my son Gary spoke about a poem of Kinnell's that he had read called "The Bear" which relates the narrative of an Eskimo who hunts a bear and finally kills it after a long trek across country, then puts on the bear's skin and drinks its blood. It is a terrible and mysterious poem that encapsulates the transformative process by which one subsumes the experience of nature to create "that sticky infusion, that rank flavor of blood, that poetry, by which I lived." Gary wondered if that last line referred to actual composition, or if "that poetry, by which I lived" was more the spiritual experience which all of us have access to in nature and which illuminates our lives.

It was a brilliant question from a thirteen-year-old and one I had not suggested. Kinnell was not forthcoming, however. His response was "That's for the reader to figure out, don't you think?" Then he closed his eyes and appeared to nod off precluding further conversation.

When we arrived at the little house on Mabel Street, Gary and I prepared dinner after showing Kinnell to his room. It was fresh trout cooked in butter and lemon, accompanied by tender asparagus, and a tomato and lettuce salad. A simple affair with a crisp Rhine wine. When we called the poet to dinner, he told us that he had eaten something on the plane and was not the least bit hungry. He just wanted to take a nap before his reading. We were disappointed and had been looking forward to a lively dinner, but we made allowances; he was, after all, a guest.

When we woke him thirty minutes before the scheduled reading, he was annoyed and belligerent, wanting to know why we hadn't awakened him earlier. I told him that the University was only a five-minute ride and that we needn't worry about parking because I would drop him off right at the door and park later. He would be there with plenty of time to spare.

He was silent and obviously annoyed most of the way there. When we arrived, he got out of the car, and my son got out as well. Gary approached the poet smiling and gave him a warm hug. "I hope you have a great reading, Mr. Kinnell. I love your poems and the audience will too!"

The reading was well-attended by university faculty, students, and a large contingent of the Tucson public. Perhaps five or six hundred people. It was a great success. As Kinnell came to the end of his performance, he paused.

"I would like to stop and recite a bit from another poem. Michael Hogan who is in the audience tonight and I both have a special affection for Walt Whitman. And I would like to share some lines from his 'Song of Myself.' I would like to dedicate this to his son Gary who gave me a hug just before the reading and wished me well."

Kinnell then went one to recite Whitman from memory. It was a very moving moment both for me and for my son. It was, in fact, a sincere and public apology for not being the ideal guest, and not being warmer with a young boy. My eyes tear up now as I remember that night and the joy that lit up my son's face as he heard his name mentioned and listened to Whitman's words recited by a true poet who indeed was transformed before us through the poetry by which he lived.

There was a child went forth everyday

And the first object he looked upon and received with wonder or pity or love or dread,

that object he became,

And that object became part of him for the day or a certain part of the day

.... or for many years or stretching cycles of years.

Affection that would not be gainsayed....the sense of what is real...

The curious wither and how....

These became a part of that child who went forth every day

And who now goes and will go forth every day

And these became a part of him or her that peruses them now.

TUCSON NIGHTS

Taking the astronomy course was not as easy as I had expected: there were several hoops to jump through. After I registered for the class, I was called to the office of the department head. He told me that he had read my request and also knew that I was a poet and a friend of his colleague Richard Shelton. He also said that while he was disposed to do a favor for a colleague and admit me, it was a class for science majors not poets. He referenced the Whitman poem(!) which he obviously didn't care for because it seemed to dismiss astronomy professors as obfuscators, and said he felt that I would struggle a great deal in the class since my background was in the humanities.

"Why do you want to take this course?" he asked.

I told him that I wanted to deepen my understanding of the universe and that I felt it would illuminate my writing. I told him of my readings of Isaac Asimov as a child and my more recent readings of Carl Sagan. I noted that, as he of course knew, Arizona had a world-renowned observatory, one of the best astronomy departments in the world, and that even the streetlights of Tucson were unique in that they were designed to eliminate light pollution so that the skies could be more carefully observed. I added that studying with his group was an opportunity that I did not want to miss.

He smiled and said that I seemed motivated. But if I really wanted to take the course, he would require that I bring to him proof that I had taken college level courses in physics and chemistry which were required. Since I did not have those courses in my transcript, I would have to take them in summer school.

It would be a long and difficult summer. As a single parent keeping a thirteen-year-old occupied, working on a directory of writing programs for the National Endowment for the Arts under Len Randolph, and doing my own freelance writing, there were some rough days. But I somehow managed to complete both courses with passing grades. I have never regretted the time or the effort, and the night skies opened to me in ways that I could never have guessed at, far more wondrous than Whitman could have imagined.

With a more thorough review of chemistry and physics under my belt, I was able to follow the lectures and explanations of how stars were born and died. We studied spectroscopy, analyzing the chemical makeup of certain stars and other heavenly bodies, and how the burning of different gasses and elements at high temperatures and the movements of a star itself, radiated light back to earth containing many shades of color along the spectrum.

I began to see how the fundamental questions of physical laws discovered on planet Earth were tested at the extremes. Astronomy deals with the entire universe, its origin and evolution. So, it also raises metaphysical questions. For example, what happened *before* the Big Bang 13.8 billion years ago when the universe came into being? Answer: there was no "before." Time and space are not separate but exist in what physicists call a time-space continuum. A single pinpoint of light expanded into matter and antimatter and caused a giant explosion, and from that came all the energy that exists.[1] Since energy can neither be destroyed nor created, only rearranged, it also created all the energy that will *ever* exist. So, "Let there be light!" is as neat a metaphor as we're likely to get for the beginning of the universe, which is as mysterious as ever even with the best scientific explanations.

I learned about the birth of comets and saw two of them clearly during my stay, one clearly with the naked eye, the other through a telescope at the Kitt Peak Observatory. I was intrigued by the enormous distances and age of the universe. It was both humbling and amazing.

What is so perfect about Tucson for experiencing all of this is that it is one of the darkest cities in the United States. In the Seventies, under pressure from university officials, local conservationists and astronomers, the city government changed all the street lighting to softer, low pressure sodium lamps, with hoods, providing reduced light pollution in the night skies. Later with the discovery of light emitting diodes (LEDs) these utilities were modified even further. Also, every evening near midnight the lights were automatically dimmed an additional thirty percent. *Basically,* joked our professor, *the only light*

---

[1] Science does not tell us how this first pinpoint light appeared. The "Unmoved Mover," or "Uncaused Cause" is never mentioned. *Ours not to reason why....*

pollution in Tucson is the full moon when it occurs. On most nights you can see the Milky Way and identify several planets and major constellations with the naked eye.

If this does not seem like a big deal, you should know that light pollution, common to all cities in the US and most developed countries today, is responsible for the global decline of flying insects, the disruption of bird migration, disjunction of plant photosynthesis, the deaths in traffic of tens of thousands of baby sea turtles, mashed on the highway instead of living a long life in the ocean which lay in the opposite direction. It also affects humans, causing sleep deprivation, cardiovascular disease, and obesity. But…back to the Milky Way which instilled in Walt Whitman the wonder that he evokes in his poem. The Milky Way today is invisible to more than 80% of the population and that number is growing.

In 1994 during a blackout in Los Angeles, the LAPD received thousands of callers on its 911 emergency line. Frightened citizens reported enormous clouds of light flashing in the sky. Some wondered if it was a nuclear explosion, others were convinced that it was an extraterritorial invasion. But the "flashing clouds" that the panicked callers saw was nothing more than (you guessed it!) the Milky Way which they were seeing for the first time! Unless more cities follow the example of Tucson's Dark Skies Initiative, and reduce light pollution, ninety-eight percent of children born in the US today will not see the Milky Way in their lifetimes.

So, this was a blessed year for me. Rather than deprive me of my sense of wonder, the astronomy course enhanced it. My studies, the lectures, observations, and visits to the Kitt Peak Observatory deepened my understanding and generated even more questions about the universe as it grew even more complex, and in the end counter-intuitive, much like the articles of faith which I learned as a child. Walking out under the night skies of the Sonoran Desert, I saw all the constellations in their brilliance that Whitman saw and like him, "I looked up in perfect silence at the stars."

It is a myth that most of the light we see is from stars that have burnt out ages ago. But it is certainly true that the stars we see now are ancient and the light from them is very old and moving away much faster than we can imagine. We can see most of the stars, constellations, and planets that the ancients saw, including the Star of Bethlehem mentioned in the Bible. Rather than one star, however, it is in fact the planet Jupiter which, at the time of Christ's birth, was in conjunction with Regulus, the crown star and, as Matthew writes in his gospel, rose in the east at the time of Christ's birth and moved across the night sky appearing to stand still near the hamlet of Bethlehem. As I write this, I am reminded of the words of T.S. Eliot writing in the Four Quartets:

> *Time past and time future*
> *What might have been and what has been*
> *Point to one end, which is always present.*

CHAPTER FIVE

JON ANDERSON AND THE FORM OF THE POEM

Jon Anderson (1940-2007) was the author of seven books of poems, and recipient of fellowships from the Guggenheim Foundation and the National Endowment for the Arts. He taught for almost two decades at the University of Arizona. His students included the poets, Tony Hoagland, David Wojahn, Michael Collier, and Agha Shahid Ali. Anderson modestly described his own work as "Certainly not for everyone. They are mostly intimate conversations with the self."

One of the things I had come to realize both as a writer and a teacher was that, while I had read a great deal of poetry, it was usually as an appreciative reader, not as a writer. As a result, I was woefully ignorant of forms besides the Shakespearean sonnet and the haiku, and was familiar with few poetic movements beyond symbolism, confessional poetry, and realism. I was also undereducated on the uses of meter, with the exception of the iambic pentameter of Frost or the heroic couplets of Pope.

So, I signed up for a course with Jon Anderson, who taught "The Forms of Poetry" in which students were required to read and then try their hand at everything from Petrarchan and Spenserian sonnets to cinquains, from haiku to limericks, from pantoums to villanelles. I don't know that any of my attempts amounted to much except for one or two sonnets and an interesting draft of a villanelle. But it gave me a new appreciation for the masters and the discipline involved. It deepened my respect for those poets whose shoulders we stand upon. Still, other bits and pieces remain which I still find useful in my own free verse poetry. I occasionally use slant rhyme, blank verse, the quatrains, and couplets of the sonnet. I have also made an interesting discovery. When I am concentrating on technical aspects in the poem, I often forget the original impulse or subject with which I began the verse. I begin to uncover something hidden which contains the seed of what the poem really wants to be about, which is often something quite different from what I originally intended or what I thought the poem was meant to convey. This element of surprise or discovery is exciting, and I hope a revelation for the reader of my poems as well, since if my expectations were confounded perhaps the reader's will be as well.

More useful, however, especially in revision, was the practice using different meters and the scanning of the lines. Scansion especially has proved to be a helpful diagnostic throughout my career as a writer. If a line limps along when I read it aloud, if it somehow misses a beat, it affects not only how the poem sounds but also changes the tone, and potentially will impede the emotional response that I hope to call forth from the reader.

A later suggestion of Anderson's when we were allowed to write in free verse, was that if a poem did not seem to be working, try scanning it and writing it in iambic pentameter or another meter. "See how the lines might change," he would tell us. "See how the meaning or the length of the line might affect both the sound and the sense."

One of the forms missing from the discussion was the prose poem. When I brought this up and suggested that it be included as part of the curriculum, Anderson asked me to explain how prose could be a poem. "I think I know what you mean but isn't it just poetic prose, and not really poetry? Maybe more like flash fiction?" he suggested. When I disagreed, he asked me to bring in some examples. So, the next week I brought in prose poems by W. S. Merwin, Robert Bly and Russell Edson. He allowed me to read them and comment on them. I took up the challenge, after a spirited defense, concluded, "So we can see by these convincing examples that poetry can be written as prose or as verse. So, it is not poetry versus prose, but rather *verse* as opposed to prose.

"Then give us your working definition of a poem, Michael," Anderson challenged.

"Well, poetry is original, concrete, and often figurative, language crafted in such a way as to evoke an emotional response. It can occur in verse or in prose."

"Even in a novel? "

"Sure, look at the *Old Man and the Sea* for example. The scene where the protagonist is hauling in the great fish and the sharks attack. He is using a handheld line, and it rips across his calloused palm deep into the soft flesh as the shark violently tugs at the fish. 'Aiii!' yells the old man. Then Hemingway writes, 'It is a word that is not translatable from the Spanish. But it is the sound a man might make, feeling the nail pass through his flesh and into the wood.'

"There we have original concrete language (nail, wood, flesh); we also have the figurative language, the allusion to the crucifixion, which creates an emotional response in the reader. Then we return to the matter-of-fact prose of the novella."

"Hmm," Anderson mused. "Would the rest of you agree with Hogan's definition of poetry here?"

A fellow student, Tony Hoagland, soon to become a well-known poet in his own right, commented. "I agree but I would add to the definition. The poem can be crafted in such a way as to evoke an emotional response, as Michael notes, or an *intellectual leap*. Sometimes a good poem can be clever or amusing, it doesn't always have to be emotional." (*Readers of poetry will note here the first hint of Hoagland's signature contribution to contemporary poetry which will be discussed in another chapter where he is the star.*)

Anderson was very generous with his tips about what worked for him as a poet and offered a number of suggestions. He said that he didn't offer explanations for the suggestions because that would mean he understood how they worked. He added that further explanation would lead to confusion and banality. Finally, he suggested that we should also treat these tips like items on a menu. Select the ones that appealed to us and ignore those that didn't.

Here are some of Anderson's tips that I copied in my notes which I have come to use from time to time in my own work. These are not direct quotes but rather notebook jottings.

- *If you find a word you like, use it. It may set the tone.*

- *Don't try to explain away the mysterious.*

- *A quiet, steady voice may be the most enduring*

- *Steal from your own poems. Keep the failures and cannibalize lines that still appeal.*

- *Read whole books, not just anthologies. Get to know another poet's voice.*

- *Follow the path the poem takes, not your preconception.*

- *Don't protect your personal life in a poem or try to justify it.*

- *Say the toughest thing.* [2]

Many of the most valuable suggestions that I use in my own drafts and revisions today, I first experimented with in this class. A few of them were already part of my tool chest. Others I adapted over time and made them my own. I also read many complete collections by other poets whom I admired, and I came to appreciate their voices and also

---

[2] There were many more of these tips. Subsequently they were collected and published in a pamphlet under the title *Helpful Hints: Notes on Writing Poetry* by Jon Anderson. Blue Moon Press, (Tucson, 1982). Sadly, the pamphlet is long out-of-print.

how they differed from my own. I had taken some risks in poems and tried to "say the toughest thing." I fought against my innate tendency to "explain" rather than just allow the poem to be. I fell in love with words.

I also realized, as T. S. Eliot, Richard Hugo, Marge Piercy had stated: competition with other poets was futile and productive of envy and rancor. My work was my own, my voice as it evolved would be unique. But I also realized (humbly, I hope, and gratefully) that I inherited a long tradition of writing and that this had been absorbed into my very being and helped me to be who I was and who I could become as a writer. It enabled me to come to the work of others with openness of mind and freshness of appreciation. It solidified my love of poetry as a reader, as well as a creator.

Jon Anderson was a lovely person, modest, unassuming, and seriously devoted to poetry. He loved to read the poems of other writers in class and refer to their work as examples. He very seldom even mentioned his own. He was a kind and gentle teacher with a quiet sense of humor. He died much too young.

CHAPTER SIX

KISSED BY ALLEN GINSBERG

I am considered a minor poet. What that means essentially is that I am not on the short list for the Harvard Visiting Writer position this year. I did not appear in Bill Moyers' video series and have not yet been invited to Breadloaf. While I appear occasionally in literary journals, including decent ones like the *Paris Review* and *APR*, my work has yet to be seen in *Harper's* or the *New Yorker*. A few textbooks and anthologies carry a couple of fortuitous poems of mine including one entitled "Spring" which has been reprinted enough to garner me sufficient royalties to buy a mountain bike.

When I die, I will join the ranks of Clough, Lovelace, Herrick and the obscure but prolific Leigh Hunt whose haunting poem "Jenny Kissed me" sums up what I love best about minor poets: their ability to hang in there as a tentative trembling note amidst the grand symphonies of Milton and Keats, Browning and Eliot. If you hang in long enough and don't embarrass too many people with your pretensions, you'll get invited places and might even be chosen to appear on stage with one of the masters to fill out a program.

It was on one such occasion, a conference of small press editors and publishers back in the late Seventies, that I first met Allen Ginsberg. The event was at California State College, which you would assume was somewhere in that eponymous state on the west coast. However, you'd be mistaken. It was actually in California, Pennsylvania, a small liberal arts college hidden in the rolling hills which border the Monongahela River.

I was a member of a trio of poets which included Dianne Wakowski and Allen Ginsberg. Our contract required each of us to give a couple of workshops to writers, editors, and graduate students during the three-day conference. Each night there was to be a poetry presentation from one of us. On Thursday night Diane would give a reading to a small group in the library; Friday, I would do the same, and on Saturday, Allen would give the final "master's" reading. I knew Ginsberg's work quite well. I had read "Howl" as a teenager. I had even taught that poem, as well as the more accessible "America" as part of my junior English class offerings in American Lit.

Ginsberg was an icon to my students, but to me he was someone more complex: a fellow war protestor whose courage I admired, a beatnik who heralded my own hippie youth, a notorious homosexual known for his forwardness. It was hard to separate the public figure from the artist. I knew that he had become part of the canon, but he was neither my favorite poet nor someone with whom I associated literary depth. He was a writer of the rant, the barbaric yawp of Whitman; one who shocked the establishment and etched a place for himself on the mutable wall of contemporary fame.

What a surprise then to attend his class on the French surrealists and to observe fellow authors, graduate students, and professors, struggling frantically to keep up with their notes as Ginsberg analyzed text, quoted lines from the poets in French, made biographical references, and connected literature to art and history. Eyes blazing above a trimmed beard, he was the epitome of a brilliant professor; not a sign of the aging beatnik to be seen. His thick lips pursed as he thought of examples to illustrate his points; his New York accent was crisp and his delivery rapid. The lecture was a *tour de force*.

That evening the three of us were invited to conduct a discussion in the round which was televised by a local PBS affiliate. We answered students' questions on the art of writing, problems with revision, the importance of close reading in literature, and the value of the masters as models. At one point a graduate student was holding forth on the feminine mystique in literature and I noted several of her classmates had begun to get that glazed look in their eyes which usually signals something less than rapt attention.

"Perhaps you should change the subject," I whispered to Allen. "I think we're losing some of our audience."

"Why don't you change the subject?" Allen replied.

"Because you have so much more authority," I said.

"Just do it, Hogan!" Allen snapped. "Show some chutzpah."

I cleared my throat and then suggested that maybe we had belabored this topic long enough. Perhaps we could turn to an earlier question, as to how a carefully chosen particular can suggest the universal.

Allen smiled, then turned and kissed me right on the lips. "Mazel tov!" he crowed.

At that exact moment, the camera, which had been focused on the student, suddenly shifted and presented the audience with the luridly thick lips of Allen connecting with my own.

Whatever the average viewer thought (or did not think) about my sexuality in those days, there was no question that my young wife of six months, who was watching the show at home, suddenly had reason for concern about my road trips. Nor was the fact that I was blushing madly as a sixteen-year-old lost on the students who sat around in the circle until one mercifully rescued me with a reply to the suggested topic change. Diane smiled knowingly, as if to say: *I am amazed at nothing men do.*

That evening Diane read from her recent book entitled *The Motorcycle Betrayal Poems* which she dedicated "to all the men who have ever betrayed me, in the hope that they will fall off their motorcycles and break their necks." It was a responsive audience, made even more so by the claque of young female groupies who sat in the front row and chuckled at her quips, applauded every poem, and added "Oh, wow!" in breathless whispers after every other verse.

The following evening, I read my poems to a group which, although more subdued and not as emotive, was no less attentive. Like Diane, I managed to sell sufficient copies of my book to ensure that next month's rent was covered. Allen, in his generous-spirited way, supported both our readings, and even stood in line until everyone else had gone before he stepped forward with his copy to be autographed. Both Diane and I were touched by that.

Towards the close of the book signing, when we were drinking wine and eating strawberry crepes, the moderator suggested that those who wished to attend the Saturday Ginsberg reading sign up now. He said that the administration was concerned about seating and wanted to make sure there were sufficient chairs in the library, so that the reading would not be interrupted by shuffling and scraping. He also said that he expected some local citizens might be attending and so would place the sign-up sheet on the library desk where it would be available throughout the following day.

As we came out of the library into the muggy Pennsylvania dark, a dozen or more buses began arriving and parking in the lot below. When they discharged their passengers, the atmosphere of the campus changed at once. Young girls wearing shorts, t-shirts and tennis shoes descended onto the tarmac and began singing scraps of songs, calling out to one another, collecting baggage and backpacks and heading to the dorms.

"They can't all be writers and editors," I remarked to Bill Welsh (aka "Grapey"), a local poet.

"Nope. It's the Eastern High Schools' Cheerleaders' Camp. Girls from all over New England came here to sharpen up their skills at cheering, tumbling, and dancing. Probably not Diane's favorite group!"

"Oh, I don't know," I said. "Some cheerleaders these days are pretty sharp. Cheerleading is more like gymnastics, much more athletic than it was in the past."

"Still, I doubt many are interested in poetry…" he observed, as the raucous groups passed us in the parking lot, shouting and chanting as they headed for the empty dorms.

I didn't disagree.

The following day, Saturday afternoon, as we went about conducting our workshops and heard their voices raised on the athletic field, I pictured them, eluding their chaperones after lights out, descending on the town's little disco and bar, dancing up a storm and tempting the local boys, then coming home a little drunk and flushed after their night out. I envisioned at least one or two sick in the bathroom, getting caught by a wide-awake coach, and threatened with expulsion from the camp. The tears, the threatened phone calls to parents….

We went out for an early dinner on Saturday evening, and then returned shortly before Ginsberg's reading was scheduled to begin. When we got to the library at 7:30 we found that it was closed. A notice on the front door informed us that, due to the size of the crowd for the reading, it had been moved to the football stadium. What? It seemed incredible that Ginsberg could draw that large a crowd of townies from a little village in the Pennsylvania woods. This we had to see!

As we headed to the stadium, we heard the din of the crowd. Not only were all the participants of the conference there and a couple of hundred folks from the town, but the entire contingent of cheerleaders as well. The open-air venue was packed with blow-dried and lipsticked teenagers, chatting away as if this was just another event in their cheerleading agenda. Incredible! And what would the aging beatnik/intellectual professor have to offer this motley crew? They seemed worlds apart.

As he strode to the stage in his dashiki and knitted yarmulke, the crowd hushed, and then burst into warm applause. The girls joined in and accompanied their applause with cheers, an occasional whistle, giggles and woos. Woos? Hmm. This will be interesting.

He played a few notes from his harmonium and then began to speak about death, the loss of his mother, the Jewish prayer for the dead. Then he read his haunting and well-known "Kaddish." The girls were quiet and respectful, as typical an audience for a poetry reading as you'd see at any college venue. Ginsberg was subdued as well. He read only a handful of poems as the evening progressed, perhaps three more of his own, a couple by William Carlos Williams, a long passage from Whitman, each piece drawing us into his inner world while opening us up to a language that was both concrete and expansive. Mostly he talked about art, about life.

And then as the hour wore down, he switched tactics. He began speaking of music, of Indian mantras, of incantatory verse and the importance of parallelism and repetition, of sound and echoes and how all of these had a spiritual essence. He talked about William Blake, the mystic, artist and poet who could write disturbing lyrics like "Tyger, Tyger," as well as simple, often sentimental Christian verses such as

"The Lamb" ("Little lamb who made thee?"). Then Ginsberg actually sang each of these poems accompanied by the harmonium: "TY-ger, TY-ger, BURN-ing BRIGHT, in the FOR-est of the NIGHT/WHAT immortal HAND or EYE, could FRAME thy FEARful SYM-atree."

The girls cheered this rendition of a poem that most of us had read at one time or another, but never actually heard sung. Ginsberg told the students that these poems were from Blake's *Songs of Innocence and Experience* and were all written to be sung. He also reminded us of the words of the Chinese poet Li Po: "Make it new! Make it new!" and said that is what poetry was all about. He connected with them personally by noting that just as their rendition of cheers and gymnastics at games "snatched beauty from the jaws of time," so, too, poets find ways to praise life that are unique while at the same time realizing that they stand on the shoulders of all those who went before and who taught us how to dance and sing. Even poetry readings like this one, he said, honor those who have gone before, remind us that all dance, all song is prayer, and that our time here is short. *Carpe diem.*

But now the stadium, that was nestled deep in a hollowed-out valley which abutted the rolling Pennsylvania hills, had begun to darken. Evening was descending and the sun blinked in and out among the trees which bordered the field. Ginsberg had waited too long to recite his well-known "Howl," a long poem which would leave him reading in the dark. It was almost time to end it. So, which one of his favorite poems would he choose? "Walt Whitman in the Supermarket"? "America"?

Now the strumming began again. And this time it was the seldom-anthologized Blake poem called the "Nurse's Song" that related the story of children playing in the fields as darkness is descending. Told by their mother that the children must be in before nightfall, the nurse calls them. But the children, wanting to take advantage of the last dying rays of the sun, are reluctant. Finally, they persuade the nurse to let them play just a little longer. The song with its haunting refrain of childhood goes like this:

> *When the voices of children are heard on the green,*
> *And laughing is heard on the hill,*
> *My heart is at rest within my breast*
> *And everything else is still.*
> *"Then come home, my children, the sun is gone down,*
> *And the dews of night arise;*
> *Come, come, leave off play and let us away,*
> *Till the morning appears in the skies."*
>
> *"No, no, let us play, for it is yet day,*
> *And we cannot go to sleep;*
> *Besides, in the skies the little birds fly,*
> *And the hills are covered with sheep."*
> *"Well, well, go and play till the light fades away,*
> *And then go home to bed."*
> *The little ones leaped, and shouted, and laughed,*
> *And all the hills echoéd.*

Now the light was fading behind the trees, and the cheerleaders all stood up the green-gold dusk as Ginsberg began the refrain a second time.

> *And all the hills echoéd, and all the hills echoéd*
> *And the little ones leaped, and shouted and laughed,*
> *And all the hills echoéd.*

Now the light voices of hundreds of teenaged girls joined him in his deep-throated amplified chorus, and the valley was filled with the sound of them, and we all rose and our voices joined in harmony chanting the ancient refrain again and again until all the hills indeed echoéd in the soft Pennsylvania evening.

Oh, if only you had been there, when we were all kissed by Allen Ginsberg.

MEMPHIS BLUES

In the summer of 1977, I was invited to do several readings of my own work: a few in the Southwest, one in Pittsburgh, another in Tennessee. In addition, I was asked by the municipal authorities to conduct a writer's workshop at the Tucson Public Library. At this venue I was to meet my second wife, Jojo Daneker, a bright and talented graduate of the University of Arizona in whom the mixture of two cultures (an Anglo officer during the War and who married a Japanese girl) gave her unique outlook on the world and a soft Eurasian beauty.

There were several highlights that summer. One of which was reading poetry at the Three Rivers Arts festival with former presidential candidate Eugene McCarthy who was also a decent poet. The other was a car trip with my son, Gary, to Memphis where we were the guests of magazine editor, Tom Daniel, and his wife, who at the time, were at the center of cultural happenings in Memphis. I gave three different readings and then, one evening in August, we had a special event at their lovely home. A quartet from the symphony orchestra were invited to play during a catered dinner of prime rib, asparagus, and buttered mashed potatoes, followed by sorbet with fresh fruit. After dinner, they played Mozart's *Eine Kleine Nachtmusik,* and I read two poems. It was quite the event of the season, and several newspaper reporters were there, as well as TV cameras from the national affiliate station. They filmed me reading one of my poems, with the quartet playing in the background. The edited clip was to be aired on the 6 o'clock news the following evening, August 16, 1977, on all their affiliates.

The next evening, as we gathered around the TV for the news, the announcer interrupted the regular show with a bulletin. We regret to inform you that the rock star, beloved crooner, and favorite son of Memphis, Elvis Presley, has just died. Presley's girlfriend Ginger Alden found the singer unresponsive on his bathroom floor in his home, Graceland. He was rushed to the hospital but then declared dead from cardiac arrest at 3:30pm.

We spent most of the evening reminiscing about Elvis. We played some of his music, and shared times when we had first heard some of his songs, including his appearance on the Ed Sullivan show when the camera showed only his upper half so the elders in the TV audience would not be shocked by his pelvic gyrations. We reminisced about dancing to "You Were Always on My Mind," "Love Me Tender," and other ballads. I was disconsolate that I had missed a moment of national fame with a clip of my poetry on the evening news, but Thom called the station manager and was reassured that they would give it an even longer airing on tomorrow's evening show. "What better time," said the manager, "to show what a cultural city Memphis is, despite the tragedy that we have suffered. We can find comfort for our grief and sorrow in music and poetry."

Unfortunately, it was not to be. The next day, crowds of mourners from all over the South and fans from up North arrived in Memphis.

They gathered around Graceland to leave tributes of flowers, teddy bears, and messages of condolence. The streets near the mansion were overflowing with locals and tourists alike. Women and men weeping openly at the loss of "the King." Suddenly, out of nowhere it seemed, a car driven by a feckless drunk plowed into the crowd. At six o'clock that evening, the news announcer presented the latest national story from Memphis which pre-empted all the other local news.

August 18, 1977: Two Monroe, Louisiana women were killed and a third was critically injured when a car being driven by a drunk 18-year-old Memphis teen, Treatise Wheeler, swerved into a crowd of over 2,000 mourners standing in front of Graceland's music gate at about 4am. Dragged and killed were Alice Marie Hovatar and Juanita Joanne Johnson, while Tammy Baiter was left seriously injured.

The driver was charged with drunk driving, leaving the scene of an accident, and two counts of second-degree murder. There would be no poetry or music that night or any other. The news cycle would move on. In the words of Virgil, *Sic volvere Parcas*, "thus the Fates spin."

CHAPTER SEVEN

COLORADO DAYS WITH REG SANER AND CZESLAW MILOSZ

Reg Sander (1928-2021) was the author of eight books of poetry and nonfiction. A combat platoon leader in the Korean War, he edited an anthology of war poetry. In his own poems his voice transcends grief and loss and appears to leave the self to merge with the unity of nature. He was the recipient of the Walt Whitman Award and a Rockefeller Foundation fellowship. From 1962 to 1998 he taught at the University of Colorado in Boulder and was that city's first poet laureate.

After a year of residencies as an Artist in the Schools working with students and communities, in Bisbee, Tucson, Phoenix, Florence, Nogales and the Sacaton Indian Reservation School, I was invited by the Colorado Humanities Program in Boulder, Colorado to set up writing workshops in the correctional facilities in Canon City. Since the base of operation was in Boulder, however, I was fortunate to spend time with two poets. One was a professor there, the other was a visiting poet and soon to be a Nobel Prize recipient.

Reg Saner, the professor, was a handsome amiable young blond fellow with a gift for teaching and an open and generously collaborative attitude toward his colleagues. Mild-mannered and gentle, he belied his past as a combat Marine. We had coffee together on several occasions, and he even suggested lesson plans for me to use with the prison inmates. One of the difficulties was that my commission involved not only the men's facility but the women's correctional center as well. The men's section was laid-back and liberal. Essentially, I was allowed to teach what I wanted, and the men felt free to discuss any issues that they had. There was no guard supervision. The women's section was much more restricted and guarded. There was always a matron supervising. Although she clearly had a genuine interest in poetry, her presence had a dampening effect on the women's willingness to share their feelings.

There were a few poems that the women had already written before I arrived, and they wanted to share them. Most were hopelessly stilted, effusively romantic, and riddled with *thee's* and *thou's* and as well as 17th century inversions: "said he", for example and "beautiful was she as the lilies." It was clear that no genuine feelings were expressed or could be in such stilted language.

Reg suggested that I not discuss their work for the first few sessions but instead bring some contemporary women's poetry and share a few examples. So, I brought some accessible and solid poems by Sharon Olds, Tess Gallagher, Marge Piercy and Denise Levertov, passed out photocopies, and read them aloud. Then we discussed why these poems worked, and what the women felt when they read them. They were amazed. "I never knew that poetry could be like this," one said. Another was abashed. "I don't know if I want to share my feelings like that." Still others saw a glimmer of possibility and by the end of the third week I was beginning to see some poems that took actual risks and that used contemporary language.

I shared my initial successes with Saner and thanked him for his suggestions. I also remarked that I had included the matron in the discussions, and she began to get caught up in the learning atmosphere of the workshop. I told him that "the next session the poems were better but…the poems have no progression. Do you know what I mean? Like in Joyce Kilmer's *Trees.* It begins with trees, there are trees in the middle, and it ends with trees."

"Ah yes, *Poems are made by fools like me but only God can make a tree.* But that's brilliant. Why not use that as an example of what a poem should *not* be: predictable, going nowhere but sticking to the central idea or image like a grade school essay. Let's find a poem we could contrast it with, I said. Maybe something from Frost."

"How about *Birches?* It is a bit difficult for a beginner, but we could take our time with it."

"A perfect example of the M&M connection!" Saner exclaimed.

"What?"

"It is what I tell my creative writing students. A good poem should have Moment and Movement. The M&M connection. There should be a moment where our attention is captured, we see something, hear something, that moves us. With Frost's poem perhaps it is the memory we all share of climbing and swinging on trees. *Ah, yes, we say. I have felt that. Been there, done that.* But before we get too comfortable, he's moved on to "ice crystals, tinkling shells," Saner said.

"Then a girl drying her hair in the sun!" I interrupted.

"Yes," Saner replied, enthused. "And then when I die "I'd like to go by climbing a birch tree toward Heaven…"

I followed with, "B*ut then dip back down again. Earth's the right place for love, I don't know where it's likely to go better.* What fun! Yes, this might work. I will bring a big bag of M& Ms for the matron as well. Perhaps she'll share them."

I know now, looking back, that in our enthusiasm we misquoted Frost but nonetheless the lesson went fine. And I was also able to revise my earlier definition of what made a good poem. I wrote in my teaching notebook: *Poetry is original, concrete, and usually figurative, language, with **moment and movement**, crafted in such a way as to evoke an emotional response or intellectual leap.*

Saner and I met often for coffee either in his office, or in the faculty lounge. Occasionally I was invited to sit in on his writing seminar and interact with the college students. He was hospitable and loved to share his passion for poetry and good writing in general. In the second semester of my tenure there, he told me he had a surprise.

"I am going to introduce you to somebody today, whom you probably do not know and haven't read. But he may be one of the most important poets in the world today."

Czeslaw Milosz (1911-2004) was born in the former Russian Empire in what is now Lithuania. He was a Polish poet, translator, and diplomat.

Threatened by Soviet authorities in 1951 he left Poland to a life of exile in Paris. In 1960 he was able to move to the US where he was a visiting professor at Berkeley. His early poems were self-translated and published in an anthology called Post-War Polish Poetry, which first brought him to the attention of American audiences. In 1980 he received the Nobel Prize for Literature.

The corridors of the liberal arts building were quiet; most of the students were in classes, I guessed. We came to an office occupied by the visiting writer and knocked. *It's open,* the resident called out. *Come in!* Inside the book-lined cubicle was a bear of a man with a full set of chin whiskers and a glint in his eye. In a thick Slavic accent, he welcomed Reg and asked who I was.

Reg introduced me as "The Irish American poet, I mentioned. Michael Hogan, fresh from the Sonoran Desert."

"So how do you like these mountains, eh? Quite a change from the desert, no?"

"Yes, quite the change," I replied smiling.

"And this, Michael, is Czeslaw Milosz, the Polish American writer, who will outshine us all in the annals of literature one day.

"Ah, careful, Reg. Remember, Eliot's caution. Between us there is no competition, only trying."

"Yes," I added. "And with worn out equipment, constantly deteriorating."

"A man after my own heart. Do you know any Polish?"

"No, I'm afraid not. I do know other Polish writers however."

"Yes?

"Umm, Zbigniew Herbert and Edward Stachura. Also, Jerzy Kosinski."

"Amazing! Well, the first, not so much so. Herbert, of course, a fine poet and many of his poems are in translation. My own poetry has not been so fortunate. All of my poems I translate myself and not so good a job. Robert Pinsky, a fine American poet, helps sometimes. Maybe you can help me and take some of my word-for-word translations and turn them into poems?

"I would be honored."

"And you know Kosinski? A captivating storyteller and a photographer. Not a poet, of course."

"Well, I corresponded with him when he was president of PEN in New York. I received a prize from that organization, and he signed off on it."

"Ah, yes. But… Edward Stachura, how on earth do you know him? He is a strange fellow, no? (He tapped the side of his head). All poets are a bit, (how do you say 'cracked'?) but he is more so than most. Perhaps the drink…."

"Well, that is how I got to know him!" I replied. "Actually, we were out drinking one night with some friends and discovered our mutual love for poetry. We traded a few lines from Federico Garcia Lorca. 'Romance Sonámbulo' was a mutual favorite.

"*Verde que te quiero verde…*" Milosz quoted.

"Exactly! Anyway, he had just returned from Mexico where he had a fellowship of some kind. Anyway, we were invited to a gala event at a hacienda owned by an important politician, maybe a governor, and it was formal. I think it was a *quinceañera* for his daughter. I had no tux, so Edward took me to a store in Nogales, and all they had that fit me was a yellow tuxedo and it was not for rent. One had to buy it. So, he was flush with funds (whether from his fellowship or whether the politician was a patron, I don't know) and so he bought me a remarkable yellow tuxedo."

"What fun! We have to find an occasion when you can wear it, right, Reg? Boulder is so dull these days with everyone so academic and serious. Of course, half the people here think I am just a political refugee and that my story is interesting for the students. Most have no idea that I am a fairly decent poet. They all want me to talk about Communism and the Solidarity Movement and Lech Walesa, yah, yah, yah. 'Oh, and did you really know Stalin?' they ask.

"I said once, *Oh you mean the man with the cockroach mustache?* They laughed then, but didn't get the allusion. Hardly anyone here reads Russian poetry, and Polish poetry even fewer."

He gave me a challenging look. And there was that glint in his eye.

"Is this a quiz?" I asked.

"Well?" he said.

"I think the reference is from Osip Mandelstam in 'The Stalin Epigram,' and later Anna Akhmatova," I said.

Milosz gave us a deep guttural laugh. "Thank you, Reg for bringing this lad by. We will meet again, Michael, I know. But now I have to run. I have a class to talk about Stalin and the old days. I think I will tell them about the Palace of Culture and Science that Stalin built. The ugliest building in Warsaw! Citizens there say, 'It may not be beautiful, but you must admit it is impressively big.' That seems to be the criterion for most architects today including those in America, don't you agree?" not expecting an answer. "Li Po said, *Make it new!* Americans and Russians say, *Make it big!*"

We spent quite a bit of time together in the following months. We went to Mass together both at the St. Thomas Aquinas Catholic Center on the campus of the University of Colorado where there was a small chapel and an intellectual priest. We also went a couple of times to the beautiful Cathedral of the Immaculate Conception in Denver (now a basilica). We both had struggles with our Catholicity. We were Catholics primarily from our families, our traditions, and shared cultural histories of oppression. Certainly the USSR in Poland and the British Empire in Ireland did what they could to stamp out Catholicism. Thus, we were bound to the faith as a form of resistance to invaders or occupiers and also as cultural inheritance. We had both been altar boys and knew Latin and loved the rituals as well, and the music, the incense, the stained glass and marble saints and the wondrous churches and cathedrals. So, there were those commonalities.

We had reservations about the hierarchy and the Church rules. The changes since Vatican II in our shared opinion made the Mass more barren, removed not only the mystery of the transubstantiation and beauty of the liturgy, but also the melodiousness of the Latin hymns, Gregorian chants, and the sense of private worship. Now there was this great communal "sharing" which neither of us liked, which seemed a cheap imitation of low church Protestant services.

We both also had a deep love of history and an understanding that it was never what the government schools and the nationalistic textbooks stated. Still...I did wonder, as I'm sure his Department of State sponsors did as well, how he could work for the USSR as a diplomat for so many years before defecting. I also wondered why, when he was a young man of thirty-three in Warsaw, he did not join the resistance movement and help fight the Nazis. Wary of jeopardizing our friendship, I postponed asking these questions for a month or more. When I finally broached the subject of the Nazis, he told me that he considered the Warsaw Uprising a lost cause and avoided participation out of self-preservation. Although he had helped several Jewish families prior to this time with money, food and hiding places.

What troubled him most about the Uprising of 1944, however, was the fact that the Russian Army was poised just outside of Warsaw and could have come to the aid of the resistance fighters, but they did not. In the end over 200,000 civilians were killed in a planned extermination slaughter by the Nazis.

"For the longest time I believed the Soviet historians who said that it was because the Russian troops were occupied elsewhere and could not be spared. But then, later in my position in the embassy, I discovered that Stalin had purposely let the Nazis destroy the city and murder civilians knowing that Poland, without an army, infrastructure, or leadership, would be a hopeless vassal of the Soviet empire. When I at last saw this report on Stalin, I knew it to be true. You are familiar, of course, with the Katyn Massacre."

"No, I'm not."

"Well, in 1940 when the Russians invaded from the north, they captured 4,800 Polish Army officers and cadets, some of the latter as young as 18. They lined them up, shot them, then buried them in mass pits in the Katyn Forest. When the Germans discovered the grave mounds and dug them up, they found the identity papers and other indications of who the victims were.

"They announced that the Russians had done this. But it was not in the interest of the Allies to admit that, so they blamed it on the Germans. The US was complicit in this coverup, not wanting to offend the Russians. Later our operatives in London found that it was the Soviets and Stalin's idea was to kill all the leadership of the Polish armed forces both present and future.

"Anyway, I began writing pieces which hinted at this history and my passport was confiscated. Also, a directive was put out by the Politburo that all writers would be under restrictions (punishable by imprisonment in Siberia) for publishing anything that did not promote the "Official History of the USSR". For a while I was trapped but then, with influence from the Foreign Minister's wife who was a friend of the family, I was able to get my passport restored and fled to France and was granted asylum.

There I was not trusted by the Polish expat community and had a difficult time. The only friend I had was Albert Camus who was very supportive and kind. Also, I had trouble getting my wife and child out of Poland. Finally, in 1960 I was offered a position at the University of California at Berkeley, and my family joined me there. But even here in America, you know, I was careful not to protest too loudly like some other professors over Vietnam and other issues because I was afraid of this government as well. And here, as you know, among academics our Catholic tradition is seen as conservative, out-of-date, and even absurd by some."

"Yes, I know," I replied." Noam Chomsky once said that '*Catholic intellectual is an oxymoron.*"

And so, our friendship grew in that brief time, but it was wary and tentative. What broke the ice was an invitation I had to attend a *quinceañera* for the niece of a Mexican American friend in Denver. The host was a civil rights lawyer and a Chicano activist by the name of Kiko Martinez. I decided to wear the yellow tuxedo to the party, and it was quite a hit. We both drank quite a bit and went to the adult party after the party and decided to stay in the city overnight. In exchange for a room and breakfast, a teacher there asked us if we would read a couple of poems for his class, and we agreed. The next morning, hungover and without another change of clothing, we both went to a school somewhere in the Mission District and Czeslaw read a couple of poems in Polish, and I read my version of them in English which I had scribbled with his help. The students (mostly Mexican Americans) seemed to have found nothing unusual for one to have a strange accent and chin whiskers, while another was decked out in a brown Stetson and a yellow tuxedo. They asked for an encore, so I read a poem or two of my own.

Not too long afterward, Milosz's wife, who had been suffering from a devastating illness, finally passed away, and he returned to California. My fellowship ended but I was soon hired by the Colorado Council on the Arts to work as a Poet in the Schools.

Eduardo, the alcoholic Polish poet whom we both admired, stumbled onto a railroad track one dark night, and was hit by a train. Although he only lost part of his hand when the train went over it, he never fully recovered and died of a heart attack a year later.

On the positive side, Milosz became great friends with Seamus Heaney who also shared his love of history, his conflictive relationship with his own country and that of a monolithic empire, as well as a complex Catholicity. I would meet Seamus at the University of Arizona in 1985 during his brief residence there and we would share many tales. I would also see Czeslaw one more time before his return to Poland at a reading sponsored by the Poetry Center at the University. It remains an indelible memory.

His opus is large and varied and critics have written hundreds of reviews and commentaries far beyond my power to add or detract. But a few lines here from "Ars Poetica?" would not be amiss. They show his sense of humor, his willingness to break the mold, and his humility.

> *I have always aspired to a more spacious form*
> *that would be free from the claim of poetry or prose*

and would let us understand each other
without exposing the author or the reader to sublime agonies.
[...]

What I'm saying here is not, I agree, poetry,
as poems should be written rarely and reluctantly,
under unbearable duress and only with the hope
that good spirits, not evil ones, choose us for their instrument.

"WHEN SORROWS COME..."

In 2010, I was asked by Dr. Bill Scotti of the US State Department if I would go to Poland to promote US education abroad. Accompanied by Maria Lesser of the College Board, I arrived in Warsaw on the evening of April 10th and was excited for two reasons. One was the opportunity to visit the major colleges in Warsaw and Krakow, including the Jagiellonian University founded in 1364, one of the oldest in the world. The second was an opportunity to visit the grave of my old friend Czeslaw and place flowers next to his sarcophagus at the Catholic Church in Skalka.

We landed on a rainy evening, dark and cold, and went to a nondescript hotel. The people we met along the way from customs clerk to the cab driver to the hotel receptionist were solemn, and unsmiling. It didn't seem like an auspicious beginning. I had just quit smoking a week or so before and was very uncomfortable in my own skin. It was after 9 PM so the coffee shop at the hotel was closed. I went to my room which was cold and uninviting so I returned to the lobby and asked if I could buy a pack of cigarettes at the front desk. The clerk said they didn't sell them. The closest place would be a pharmacy three blocks away.

I went outside. It was cold and windy. Two rather unattractive prostitutes were slouched in front protected by the hotel's awning from the rain. They were both smoking. I thought briefly about approaching them and caging a cigarette, then changed my mind. It might lead to a solicitation that I had no appetite for. I went back inside, crawled into the cold bed, tossed fitfully for a while; the sheets felt damp and uncomfortable. It took me a very long time to finally go to sleep.

Our first meeting the next morning was at 9 am with members of the Cabinet and the First Lady at the Presidential Palace. When we arrived at Palace Square there were metal police barricades and armed soldiers. Outside the restricted area were dozens of cameramen and reporters from BBC, CBS, RTE, ARD, ZDF and other news outlets from around the world. We listened in as the BBC broadcaster gave his report. *The president is dead, along with the First Lady and 92 others including senior military officers from all services, the deputy foreign minister, twelve members of the Polish Parliament, and others.*

The others, we later discovered, included the relatives of the victims of the Katyn Massacre of 1942 when Stalin ordered the deaths of all the young Polish officers and cadets who were then buried in a mass grave in the Katyn Forest. Now their siblings and children, who had come to mourn, were also dead, after the Presidential plane that was carrying them crashed outside of Smolensk, Russia. They had gone to participate in a solemn memorial of the young victims of mass executions which the Russian government had now belatedly acknowledged. I was reminded of the world of Claudius in *Hamlet,* "When sorrows come, they come not in single spies, but in battalions."

This, it would turn out, was not hyperbole. More sorrows were yet to come.

We presented our credentials, including our confirmation of the meeting at the Palace with a young soldier stationed at one of the many barricades. He returned with an army captain who asked for our passports. He took those as well and went to the person who I assumed to be in command who communicated with officials in the Palace. Minutes later the barriers opened a crack to let us in and we were escorted to the Great Hall. Beneath a large historic oil painting, a massive buffet was laid out with a silver coffee urn, a tea service, a large ham, a side of beef, assorted breads, cheeses, and juices. There were also several dignitaries present, including the Minister of Culture and the Minister of Foreign Affairs, who were seated at an ornately carved wooden table toward the front of the hall. They all rose and were presented to us by the Deputy Prime Minister who made us welcome. He voiced his regrets that the First Lady could not be there. International education was a commitment "dear to her heart," he said. He added that despite the tragedy that had recently befallen the country, it was important to honor visits such as ours, and he hoped that we could all work together to provide more opportunities for the young people of Poland.

I then expressed the condolences of Maria and myself on behalf of the US government, unaware at the time of the significance of my words and our presence there. He invited us to accompany the other dignitaries on the funeral train scheduled to leave April 18th to Krakow where the President and First Lady would be interred in the famous Wawel Castle chapel.

On April 14, as if nature herself conspired to deepen grief, a major volcano erupted in Iceland. It emitted clouds of volcanic ash so thick and high that it endangered all aircraft in Europe. So, neither President Obama nor any other major western leader was able to fly to Poland for the funeral. We would be the only US representatives who had come to the country and expressed our condolences during this tragic episode.

CHAPTER EIGHT

STEVE ORLEN AND PERMISSION TO SPEAK

Steve Orlen (1942-2010) was an American poet, author of seven books, whose work also appeared in well-known journals and several anthologies. He was a much beloved professor at the University of Arizona where he was the cofounder of the renowned Creative Writing Program.

When I returned to Arizona on a graduate fellowship after my sojourn in Colorado, I was pleased to meet up with Steve Orlen. Not only was he a poet who I much admired, but over the years we became friends. He was the co-founder of the MFA Program at the University of Arizona and had invited me to become a part of the program several years earlier. But then I had a family to support, a new wife who was pregnant, and a job offer in another state. Now, I was at loose ends again and was grateful to be re-invited to the program. It was relatively new and highly selective. I believe there were only twelve or so in my group and he promised a teaching assistantship and that was a deciding factor.

Being in Steve's poetry seminar was a genuine treat for me. In addition, in those days before the internet, we exchanged letters from time to time and occasional phone calls. We were both interested in the narrative and finding ways to expand it. Sometimes it might be recalling a chance remark, or a scrap of memory, then creating a story which might flow from that with its own mysterious revelations, as Frost put it, "like a piece of ice on a hot stove might ride to its own melting."

One piece of his which we dismantled and discussed in class was also the title poem of his book, *Permission to Speak*, the cover of which was illustrated by his wife, Gail. The poem recounts a story of a man in a village, perhaps in Russia, looking out at a gray stand of birch and hickory. Powered by a nearby river is a mill which grinds flour. Tomorrow the man will eat the bread. It had snowed during the night and the countryside was blurred in a frosty mist…then the man had a waking dream.

> *After a spring snow a father and son*
> *took a sleigh ride along the riverbank*
> *And what the son couldn't see*
> *the particular hills and trees lost to whiteness*
> *made him cry.*
> *The father snapped the reins and pointed out*
> *what must have been a red fox sliding past a birch.*
> *"Look at the fellow in the bright nightgown!"*
> *From which the son will date his love of the world*
> *traveling softly past.*

After I gave my own analysis of the poem, and how I thought it was crafted, Steve surprised me.

"Well, there was no father and son meeting. I imagined that. Or perhaps I was dreaming. And I don't know anything about mill towns in Russia, although I grew up in Holyoke, Massachusetts, which had a textile mill and then several paper mills in the 19th and early 20th centuries. And of course, there was the Connecticut River and really cold winters and heavy snows, so all those memories are there. Also, the birches and the hickory. Even the sleighs. I rode on one pulled by a horse when I was in junior high. I think some kid's grandfather owned it."

"How about the business of the fox and the bright nightgown."

"Ha! You liked that, hey? I stole the line from W. C. Fields. He used it as a metaphor for death. Although I don't think it means death, exactly, in this poem. Although maybe it could."

That was Steve. Stealing a line from a comedian of his grandfather's era, making up a "memory" out of whole cloth. And by sharing all this, opening imaginative possibilities for me as a poet. It was an example of what Sam Hammill termed "the gift economy." But that was not all. He said he had gotten the idea for the poem from another poet and fellow professor at the University, Norman Dubie, during a conversation they had.

What was so delightful and charming about Steve was his candidness, his willingness to acknowledge his sources, his sense of humor, his celebrations, his borrowings from classics as well as contemporaries, and his zest for life.

"Poetry is really about life, right? Like Frost said, *a love affair with life*. Maybe sometimes even helping us how to live it fully, even though we never quite manage it. So, our lives consist of creating something out of the mess we've made."

On another occasion, he said that a poem should come out of a desire to ask questions, not provide answers. "A successful poem leads the reader *and the writer* to an altered awareness." This was why Steve encouraged writing often, keeping scraps of failed poems, questions, vague memories, odd quotes and descriptions in a notebook so that one might access the unconscious in a moment of reflection, and occasionally find a way to create something new out of the mundane scraps and pieces.

There are some poems that I return to again and again not merely because I have not yet exhausted their possibilities but also because they are emotional touchstones whose resonances continue to move me. T.S. Eliot's "Dry Salvages," James Wright's "A Blessing," Jaime Sabines' "Luna," Anna Akhmatova's "Requiem" and Steve Orlen's "Permission to Speak" top the list, which includes about a hundred poems that I have re-read with family, friends, students and-quite often-in solitude over the years.

The handful of books that Orlen wrote over the years contain carefully burnished poems with a unique narrative voice that is wry, intimate and tough. His last book, *A Thousand Threads*, is even more melodious. The rich vein of sex that he has exploited better than any of his contemporaries is present there, as is the mordant wit and the classic narrative opening. But there's something more. These are mature poems, but they still have the freshness of early Orlen where childhood memory revives itself in the present and illuminates a moment that feels transcendental for the reader. There is a tuneful blending of language and music, which makes the narrative lyrical and stops the story line short or turns it (tunes it) to another melody. One of my favorites is "Hurricane."

When the father says, Think before you speak, it's like telling a clown
To be serious for once. Like telling an actor to freeze long moments on a stage
And reconsider the lines he's memorized. Like telling the color yellow
To tone it down for the funeral. The boy is eleven. It's hard to think
With that noisy rain still coming down in buckets. Last night a hurricane
Slammed the street and in the morning the boy's uncle stopped by
In a canoe, waving a paddle, and the big trees were upended, everyone
could see what made a tree a tree.

"To remain alive in this world requires careful attention," Steve once said. He followed his own prescription. His poems which flow so freely, so lyrically, also have the incisive clarity of pizzicato, each note precisely plucked by an attentive and careful musician.

The "Hurricane" excerpt just quoted is a prose poem which reminds me of a bit of gossip I heard about Steve back in the Sixties when he was at a writers' conference with Kurt Vonnegut. I should say here, lest someone question my sources or my motivations, that Steve loved gossip, especially about other writers. Not malicious tales, but ones that were interesting or amusing. The following tidbit I first heard from Michael Collier, which was later embroidered by Joseph Brodsky and was never denied by Steve himself.

It seems that after a writer's conference Steve and Vonnegut repaired to a local tavern. There they were discussing writing and literature, and Steve mentioned something about the prose poem. "There's no such thing," Vonnegut asserted. "It is a contradiction in terms."

"Not really," Steve replied. "Verse and prose may be a contradiction but not prose and poetry necessarily. It has a long history with the French: Mallarmé, Baudelaire, Rimbaud."

"Effeminate fakers, fraudsters, anyone who subscribes to that crap is an idiot." replied Vonnegut, already in his cups.

"Even many respected contemporaries," Steve replied. "For example, Bly, Edson…"

"Total bullshit! Fake art! You are such an asshole!"

Steve persisted. He was actually practicing this art himself and was not about to concede to someone whom he considered to be acting like a Philistine.

"Bashō in 17th century Japan, Marash of Syria, Jean Paul of Germany."

"Hope you are not teaching that crap, Orlen. I can't believe they actually pay you for shit like that. Total crap! Stupid, simplistic shit!" spraying spit on Steve, who responded with a quick left to the gut of his adversary that left Vonnegut breathless.

Both were asked to leave the bar. Or so the story goes. As I said, Steve never denied it and, of course, he had mellowed a great deal since then. Unlikely to land anyone a blow to the stomach or the jaw when I worked with him, he still had a bit of the bad boy from the New England mill town about him.

Steve had the gift of making one comfortable in his presence. If you were a committed writer, he was probably the most useful creative writing teacher on the staff. But he was not proactive, nor particularly helpful in providing prompts, as Jon Anderson was, for example. On the other hand, if you did produce something workable for his review, he was brilliant at showing you why it "almost" worked, diagnosing flaws, and suggesting remedial measures.

Steve and I became good friends, and as the semester drew to a close, he said that he was going on sabbatical and wanted me to take over his class. It was an honor. But there was also a warning. While Steve was always upbeat and never made you feel small, with slackers he could be ruthless. This is why he was both praised and disparaged in student evaluations. He could be demanding and sometimes made critical statements that were unequivocal and barbed. Once when I failed to turn in an assignment for his class two sessions in a row, he told me quietly, "Michael most writers fail, not for lack of talent, but for lack of character." Fortunately, I did not let Steve down when I took over his classes. My addictions had abated for a time. I was creative, enthusiastic, and had a good rapport with the students. But his comment came to haunt me the following year as periodic drinking bouts caused me to miss appointments and deadlines until I finally decided to get on the road to recovery.

Envoi

It was a privilege to visit with Steve in 2010, shortly before his death from lung cancer. He gave me an inscribed copy of his latest book and I gave him one of mine. We talked about old times. As always, we chatted about poetry and poets. I was telling him about my exchanges with the poet William Stafford and an incident that opened up for me a way of living that I had not thought about before. He smiled and said, "Yes, I have had the same experience. Often reading a poem, or talking with a fellow poet, I become aware of a way of living that I had not fully considered before. Poetry has helped me live."

I think it may have helped him to die as well when that fatal day arrived. Maybe that's the way to be in the world and then leave it gracefully, more in love with it for all the people we've known. Steve spent his last afternoon with his friends and former students in his shaded garden in Tucson sharing memories. That evening, resting after a long day, he turned to Gail and with a smile said, "Enough," and then let go.

CHAPTER NINE

A BREATH OF FRESH AIR WITH EDWARD ABBEY

Edward Abbey (1927-1989) was an American essayist, novelist, and environmental crusader. Author of more than thirty books, he was a cult figure for a whole generation of nature writers and activists.

Appearing more like a rancher than a professor, Edward Abbey strode into our evening class in a pair of scuffed boots, faded Levi's, and a plain blue cotton shirt. His lanky hair was mashed down by a sweat-stained cowboy hat of dubious pedigree. He sported a curly beard which was not quite full length nor trimmed. He introduced himself as an itinerant scribbler, lover of nature, and anarchist. "If that last term offends you, then prepare to be uncomfortable in this class. I tend to have as little as possible to do with our government, or any other for that matter. I do not compete for grants or fellowships and will take only a minimum wage from the Park Service when I work as a fire lookout in the summers."

The name of the course he was allegedly teaching was "Creative Nonfiction," a relative newcomer to the curriculum. Probably suggested by a few recent works including Truman Capote's *In Cold*

Blood, Tim O'Brien's *The Things They Carried,* the work of gonzo journalists, like Hunter S. Thompson, and the English Department's pursuit of the current trends.

I had read one excellent book by Abbey called *Desert Solitaire,* which was and remains today probably the best book about the American outback ever written. So, I had a special affinity for him from the start. He was, however, a wildly erratic teacher. His "assignments" often appeared bizarre to many of the upper-class kids who never strayed far from their family 's backyards. He instructed us to go into the desert on the weekend and take notes for a field guide. He assigned anarchist and anti-government essays for homework. He played the original Victrola version of "This Land is Your Land" which included Woody Guthrie railing at the "No Trespassing" signs which even in the era of the Dust Bowl signaled the enclosure of the West. He gave us scientific articles to read on water usage and dam construction.

Lest one think Ed would be classified as a leftist or progressive in current terms, one should know that he once spent a whole period lambasting the idea that immigration from Mexico and Central America was in any way a good idea for the republic or, more importantly, for the environment.

What concerned him most was that America had reached a point in its development where it could no longer afford the lavish expenditure of water, depletion of fertile land and clean air. Nor could it continue indefinitely intensive corporate agriculture, building more high-rise apartments, endless consumerism, and reckless consumption of energy and production of waste.

"The capitalist system is like a snake eating its tail," he went on to tell us. He believed it was structured so that it could survive only if there was continual growth and that is measured by the gross national product. However, it did not take into consideration the expenditure of the planet's limited resources which were not growing exponentially like the economy and our consumption. The resources were static and were being depleted more each day this out-of-control expenditure was taking place.

"Unlimited growth," Abbey asserted, "is the etiology of the cancer cell. And its ultimate result is the destruction of the host."

He was not a racist or someone who felt immigrants were somehow inferior or taking citizens' jobs, nor did he cotton to the "replacement theory" so popular with Republicans today. His argument was entirely environmental and had to do not only with America's future but the life of the planet. I would paraphrase it like this:

We Americans use about a third of the energy in the world today. A country like Guatemala, less than one percent, where a good part of the workforce is engaged in sustainable farming. The farmer works a small plot with maybe a cow for milk, a few chickens for eggs and an occasional roast, and a lush vegetable garden from which he can often sell the surplus for small amounts of cash, or trade for cloth which his wife will sew into dresses and overalls. He supports his family, sees that they are fed and clothed, and has a negligible negative impact on the planet.

But let him come north and become a part of the dollar economy, and he will soon be using fossil fuel to excess just like the rest of us, heating his house, driving his car, and increasing the expenditure of energy and nonrenewable resources that have made America the biggest polluter in the world. Multiply this by the hundreds of thousands, even millions who want to immigrate, and you have a recipe for planetary disaster.

Abbey certainly got us out of our comfort zone and forced us, regardless of our ideals or family upbringing, to re-think everything we had been taught or believed about our society and our American way of life. I can't remember any prolonged argument in class, but there were often voices of dissent, which he welcomed and told the dissenters to write down their views. He felt that righteous anger and outrage were natural impulses that should not be repressed by a teacher or anyone else, but should be written down carefully, considered with an open mind, and then supported by statistics and evidence, not merely spewed out in an emotional reaction.

Abbey was a breath of fresh air to some, an inflammatory spark to others, and a dangerous radical to a small minority. Some would go on to become activists, such as the "Eco Raiders" who chained themselves to trees in the forest to prevent lumber companies from clear cutting. Others would disable earth moving vehicles meant to dig ditches for dams or other construction projects in or near formerly protected areas. Some joined the Park Service in the summers and became lifelong supporters of environmental concerns. Some became naturalist writers whose works now grace contemporary magazines. Still others,

I suspect, reported him to the dean or the Board of Regents. At any rate, I don't remember seeing his name in the course catalog in later years and, when I recount my days with him among young teachers today, many are amazed that he was allowed to teach at all.

Those who knew him well were loyal to him even as he struggled through his last days during the Ides of March of 1989. Suffering from esophageal bleeding after an unsuccessful surgery, he was asked by those gathered at his bedside what last words he would want to be remembered by. Irascible and irrepressible up to the end, he replied, "No comment." Then he quietly passed on.

He had earlier expressed a wish that his body be snatched from whatever funeral home or other place it was taken and be transported to the desert in a pickup truck. He wanted to be buried in the desert, without embalming, in an old sleeping bag. He asked that friends and family celebrate his death with a case or two of beer and some raucous singing. "I prefer no funeral oration," he reportedly told his brother-in-law. "However, I will not interfere if someone would like to say a few final words."

His wishes were followed. His remains are in a grave somewhere in the Cabeza Prieta Wilderness in the Sonoran Desert. Inscribed on a nearby stone are the words: "Edward Paul Abbey. 1927-1989. No Comment."

CHAPTER TEN

HANGING OUT WITH VETERANS: TONY HOAGLAND AND AGHA SHAHID ALI

When we joined the Creative Writing Program as fellows at the University of Arizona, three of us already had degrees from other institutions and were published writers. Two became close friends of mine: Tony Hoagland and Agha Shahid Ali. We were all over thirty, considerably older than our classmates. We had all attended several universities, and had degrees, including a law degree (me) and a PhD (Shahid). We had all worked multiple jobs from fruit picking to construction, from private tutoring and law clerking. It was natural that we formed a cadre within the program to support each other, share ideas and teaching practices, and read each other's work-in-progress. I think our distinguishing characteristic in the class was how well-read we were. If one is at all interested in literature, one has developed a much wider reach and depth of reading by their mid-thirties than the average twenty-one-year-old.

Tony Hoagland (1953 –2018) was an American writer. He was the author of eight poetry books, three books of critical studies, and a dozen broadsides and chapbooks. He received numerous awards for his work, including two NEA fellowships and a nomination for the National Book Award. A popular teacher and public reader, he was noted for his humor, his love of language and his mordant wit.

I think the word "cadre" is a useful one to describe the three of us, because ours was much like a law school study group where one member might have a bit more knowledge of tax law, another, criminal law, a third, constitutional law. And each one shared his expertise. Tony was interested in humor, diction, and voice. His own voice was unique, not because he went about consciously inventing it but because he read so widely that he really discovered a way of *not* writing. *Not like this one, more like this one, but not exactly.* So, while he emulated many writers, he found none of their voices quite satisfactory for his own poems. He felt that the writers at the University of Iowa took themselves too seriously and read poets who, in the main, were dark or had a reactive and often depressing view. That, of course, was one way of going and a valid one. But not for Tony. He had studied Buddhism and wanted to find a way of writing that would accept the world as it was with all its messiness, find the humor in it, and examine the contradictions. This did not in any way diminish his moral vision of life as it should be lived, or how a society could be more humane. In fact, it brought those concerns to the forefront of his readers' consciousness regardless of their religion or lack of it, their politics, their lifestyles.

In his poem "America," he is critical of a student who, with purple hair, shouts with a gang of friends ("letting rap music pour over them/Like a boiling Jacuzzi full of ball peen hammers") that life in America is like "living in a maximum-security prison." He wants to tell the kid "how full of shit he is," that he is clueless and asleep. But he forebears. Instead, he turns inward and reflects.

> *…I look at the student with his acne and cell phone and phony ghetto clothes*
> *And I think, "I am asleep in America too,*
> *And I don't know how to wake myself either."*
>
> *And I remember what Marx said near the end of his life:*
> *"I was listening to the cries of the past,*
> *When I should have been listening to the cries of the future."*
>
> *But how could he have imagined 100 channels of 24-hour cable*
> *Or what kind of nightmare it might be*
> *When each day you watch rivers of bright merchandise run past you*
> *And you are floating in your pleasure boat upon this river*
> *Even while others are drowning underneath you*
> *And you see their faces twisting in the surface of the waters*
> *And yet it seems to be your own hand*
> *Which turns the volume higher?*
> ("America")

"I could never imagine using *boiling Jacuzzi full of ballpeen hammers* in a poem," I told him.

"But does it work?" he asked.

"Yes, yes, of course. But I'm not sure why."

"Well," Tony said, "I think it might have to do with a choice of diction, where I wanted that poem to go. I wanted it to reach those of us who equate tolerance with acceptance. Those who think that liberalism means tolerating all kinds of bull. Folks who believe that ugliness is part of the social fabric, and we should just let it slide.

"I think as writers, as educators, we need to point out, in clear uncertain terms, in ways that reach out to students who are dying their hair ugly colors, wearing clothes convict-style with their butts hanging out, listening to rap music that denigrates women and paying $30 for an album that suggests killing cops is a good idea, that all this is *not* rebellious counterculture. They need to know that they are really buying into a fake subculture which has already been hijacked by the corporations. They are not resisting consumerism; they are adding more flavors to it."

"Wearing clothes convict-style?"

"Yeah, when you go to jail, they take your belt away, causing your pants to droop. That's the origin of that below-the-butt look!"

We were to have more conversations about diction but one truth that stayed with me and has since been reinforced over the years by the psychology of William James is that diction has a cumulative effect. It can be used not only to pinpoint meaning but also to invoke a whole resonating web of conceits and ideas.

But I think what Tony and I both liked about his poem was the discovery that he (and the reader) made about themselves. They are part of the consumer culture as well and are contributing to it in as many negative ways as the clueless teenager. That is humbling.

We had both read widely in Latin American Literature and knew about Pablo Neruda's exile and the role Henry Kissinger and the CIA played in overthrowing a democracy in Chile and installing a military dictator. We knew about American support of the Contras, the invasion of Grenada, the crushing of dissent by US trained rightwing militias. We understood how our country had usurped the word "America" from its continental significance and applied it exclusively to one nation. So, when Octavio Paz wrote, "I look forward to the day when the US becomes just a part of the Americas," we knew what he meant. Tony wrote:

> *It's going to be great when America is just a second fiddle...*
> *Old men reading the Times on a bench in Central Park*
> *will smile and say, Let France take care of it.*
>
> *America...when you pound your chest like that in public*
> *It just embarrasses us...*
>
> *I'm learning to say I'm sorry in more and more foreign*
> *languages.*
>
> ("Ode to the Republic")

Meanwhile, according to Tony, we continue to vote warmongers into office, choose not to form an anti-war party (nor even add a plank to the platforms of either the Republican or Democratic parties that opposes preemptive war). We never reached out to protest the unconscionable defense budget, while lavishing fake praise on our volunteer troops and contract mercenaries, thanking them "for their service" as they made the world safe for exploitive technologies and bloated corporations, while supporting tyrants in oil-rich nations, and degenerate arms producers at home and abroad. There was nothing self-righteous or smug in Tony's moral positions. Nor virtue signaling either. Just a clear-headed look at who we are, a little yellow canary in the coal mine.

I miss Tony every day. He died too young. He was bright, passionate, and funny. He always had a refreshing way of looking at life. Even the bleakest day had some sunshine when Tony was around. The shit of the world was a compost pile for him in which flowers grew. Often with thorny brambles like the Scotch Thistle, but flowers as well that were, as Robbie Burns might say, still quite "bonny for a' that."

Speaking of scatological language, I remember one day coming late to Orlen's writing seminar and there was a new student at the table. He appeared quite young, with a baby face, although I was to learn that, like Dick Clark, he merely had that handsome, ageless look, even though he was quite a bit older than anyone else in the group. Anyway, Orlen was saying, "While I don't entirely agree with what shithead was saying, I do see his point."

How odd, I thought. Orlen is usually unfailingly polite. I had never heard him call a student by an insulting name before. As the discussion ensued, I heard again, "Yes, yes. But isn't that actually what shithead was saying? I find it to be a bit exaggerated."

When we had a break, I went up to Steve and said, "Who is this new guy, and why do you call him 'shithead'? That's really not cool, Steve?"

"What are you talking about, Michael? Do you mean Shahid."

"Huh?"

"His name is Agha *Shahid* Ali, he's from India."

"Oh, sorry," I said, feeling a bit like Rosanne Rosana-dana from Saturday Night Live.

Agha Shahid Ali (1949-2001) was born in India and immigrated to the United States. With degrees from universities in India and the US, including a PhD from the University of Iowa and an MFA from the University of Arizona, he was part of the New Formalism movement in poetry. A recipient of the Guggenheim fellowship and the Pushcart Prize, he published six volumes of poetry and three books of translations and was a finalist for the National Book Award.

When I found out his age (closer to forty than twenty) I thought of Dorian Gray and wondered if perhaps this strikingly handsome Adonis did not have a moldering portrait somewhere in his attic. He was easy to like, and we hit it off very early on. We both shared a love for the poetry of T.S. Eliot, not so much the experimental stuff like "The

Hollow Men" but the more formal "Four Quartets." Like me, Shahid had memorized portions of "Dry Salvages" and other lengthy verses and could recite them at the drop of a hat. He also shared my love for narrative poetry and for puns and paradoxes. I had no idea that this was part of any school of poetry, or that it might be considered what is now termed "neo-formalism." I just enjoyed it.

I also liked the variety of injecting a feminine rhyme here and there as well as writing the occasional poem in strict iambic pentameter, which I knew was a throwback to Frost. But I first came upon it, not as a device, but as a suggestion from Jon Anderson. He proposed that when a line seemed to be clunking, when the poem did not "sing," or have a certain music to it, that I try scanning it, and seeing if there might be a meter which would lend itself to both sound and sense. So. There we were, many afternoons and evenings over many cups of tea for him and beers for me discussing our work, oblivious to the world around us.

For Shahid, the rhyme was usually planned, especially when he chose a form such as the Petrarchan sonnet and the *ghazal*. The latter is an Arabic form which harkens back to his upbringing as a Muslim. But he wrote in English, which sometimes echoed his Catholic school education both in imagery and in allusions. The *ghazal* consists of verse in rhymed couplets with sometimes a refrain. It is usually about loss, or unrequited love.

Occasionally, Shahid kept to the form strictly; other times he played with it or altered it.

The theme of loss is often present in his most evocative poems, as are the couplets which are characteristic of much of his verse. Still, for all his formalism, Shahid could often open up the poem in unexpected ways and make it feel much more a part of where he was living, than any ancient Arabic land or even his homeplace in India

> On January 19, 1987,
> as I very early in the morning
> drove my sister to Tucson International,
>
> suddenly on Alvernon and 22nd Street
> the sliding doors of the fog were opened,
>
> and the snow, which had fallen all night, now
> sun-dazzled, blinded us, the earth whitened
>
> out, as if by cocaine, the desert's plants,
> its mineral-hard colors extinguished,
> wine frozen in the veins of the cactus....
>
> And we are driving by the ocean
> that evaporated here, by its shores,
> the past now happening so quickly that each
>
> stoplight hurts us into memory, the sky
> taking rapid notes on us as we turn

> *at Tucson Boulevard and drive into*
> *the airport, and I realize that the earth*
>
> *is thawing from longing into longing and*
> *that we are being forgotten by those arms....*
>
> *that I would lose,*
> *of all that I was losing.*
>
> *("Snow on the Desert")*

Just before we left Tucson for the last time, Shahid came by our house to bid us farewell. He was a great cook and brought some *lyde*, which is a Kashmiri dessert made by frying whole wheat flour. It has kind of a neutral taste but, when dipped in Sheer Chai tea (which he also brought), could be quite tasty. We exchanged some recent poems with each other, talked a bit about both our teaching positions, and he spoke seriously with my son about his reading and his education. Teaching was his passion.

When he got up to leave, my son embraced him with tears, and I followed. He was a good friend. I did not know that it would be the last time we would meet. He died of brain cancer a month after the fall of the Twin Towers in 2001.

The Pakistani novelist Kamila Shamsie, Shahid's creative writing student in the 90's, recounts the story that some months after he was diagnosed with brain cancer, Shahid was riding the subway going to teach his class at NYU when he started to feel faint and began to black out. 'For a moment, 'he thought, "I'm dying," and then he told himself, "No. First I'll teach my class, then I'll die."'

CHAPTER ELEVEN

FROM PRISON TO YALE: JIMMY SANTIAGO BACA, POET OF THE BARRIO

Jimmy Santiago Baca (b.1952—) is a poet, screenwriter and memoirist. He is the author of books in several genres, and the recipient of many distinctions and awards. He wrote, acted in and produced the cult classic film Blood In, Blood Out.

He speaks to thousands of young people at high schools and college campuses, as well as to mature audiences in bookstores and libraries. He was appointed to a prestigious professorship at Yale University. He has received the Hispanic Heritage Award for Literature, the American Book Award for Poetry, the Pushcart Prize, and is the author of eleven volumes. His popularity crosses age and racial lines, and he has been translated into a dozen languages. Jimmy Santiago Baca, Poet of the People.

Yet, Baca came to poetry from a place of despair and total darkness. Born in Santa Fe, New Mexico in 1952, abandoned by his parents at age two, a runaway from an orphanage at age thirteen living in the street, young Baca turned to drugs and ended up serving time in the notorious

Arizona State Prison in Florence. He was put into the bleakest of maximum-security cell blocks, built by inmates from the Territorial Prison in 1908, four years before Arizona became a state. Here, amid overcrowded conditions, daily stabbings, and vermin-infested quarters, he came across a tattered poetry anthology left by a departing inmate. He remembers: "Slowly I enunciated the words,...p-o-n-d, rip-ple...I always thought reading was a waste of time, that nothing could be ever gained by it. Even as I tried to convince myself that I was merely curious, I had become so absorbed in how the sounds created music in me and happiness, I forgot where I was... then I looked at the name, a poet called Wordsworth."

Thus began Baca's hunger for beauty and his passion to write his own words, a compulsion which burned within him. "When at last I wrote my own words on the page, I felt an island rising beneath my feet like the back of a whale." He was on his way. He sent a few pieces out to *Rolling Stone Magazine* and then-editor Denise Levertov remarked on his talent. It was the beginning. She mentioned him to Richard Shelton, who was then conducting workshops at the Arizona State Prison. Baca was unable to attend in person because he was in a Segregation cell for his own protection when he refused to join a prison gang. Nevertheless, he began corresponding with Shelton, sending him poems, and asking for comments. Jimmy would become one of Shelton's most successful students. My wife Lucinda and I met Jimmy shortly after his release, at a poetry festival in Oakland, California. We took Jimmy to dinner and afterwards accompanied him to one of his first public readings since his parole from prison. The event was well-attended with a large group of Mexican Americans coming to see him make good, but Jimmy was nervous, and his voice was flat, without inflection or emphasis. Fortunately, the poems that he chose to read were accessible and full of imagery that the crowd could relate to. One that was quite popular with the crowd was a love poem.

> *I am offering this poem to you,*
> *since I have nothing else to give.*
> *Keep it like a warm coat,*
> *when winter comes to cover you,*
> *or like a pair of thick socks*
> *the cold cannot bite through....*
>
> *It's all I have to give,*
> *and it's all anyone needs to live,*
> *and to go on living inside,*
> *when the world outside*
> *no longer cares if you live or die;*
> *remember,*
> *I love you. ("I am Offering This Poem")*

After the reading, Lucinda presented Jimmy with a beautiful quilt she had made. It was titled *Tithonus*, after the lover of Eos, the goddess of light. A reminder that Jimmy had been brought out of the darkness to the light of love and freedom. It graces the wall of his New Mexico home today.

In 1983 when Baca's early poems began appearing in major literary magazines, I was asked to write a piece for *the American Book Review* on his first collection. I was impressed but also cautious. I noted at the time that Baca was a remarkable new talent who wrote powerful poems with disarming ingenuousness. His passion was obvious. His work reminded me a bit of the late Dylan Thomas who was often described as "word-drunk" because his images came so fast and furious. Jimmy was a natural poet with a remarkable gift for image-making. But I also lamented a certain looseness, and a tendency for overwrought emotion. I wrote, "I look forward to his next, more polished volume."

I was not disappointed. In 1987, he published *Martin and Meditation on the South Valley,* which was mature, tightly crafted, with the powerful emotions still there but understated which made them even more evocative. He received the American Book Award for this volume. It became popular with people from all walks of life and made him an instant folk hero in his native New Mexico. Baca was invited to be a guest on several radio and television programs, including National Public Radio's *All Things Considered, Good Morning America*, CBS Sunday Morning, and *Language of Life* with Bill Moyers.

He followed this book with *Black Mesa Poems* in 1989, which reflected his coming to peace as he settled in with his wife and two children on a small New Mexico ranch. Now in demand across the country for poetry readings and lectures, he also wrote a script for a hit movie, *Blood In, Blood Out,* and had his poems performed by everyone from high school students in "Poetry Out Loud" competitions to practiced narrators and musicians on YouTube. Here is another excerpt from a Baca poem that has been proven very popular especially with young students and that I have used in my own classes when working in California and Colorado with the Poets in the Schools Program.

As a niño I believed
God carved my grandfather in a few minutes.
He was rough-cut—
thick-knubby field working hands
his face a ball of maiz dough
wind and sun fingers had kneaded
into a calm, bronzed, kind face....

In the distance
I could hear someone chopping wood,
and smell the heat wavering off stones
and sense the loneliness that brimmed
from adobe houses at dusk

A loneliness
no one could see, that I sensed
in a horse's tail,
a cow's glum look, or the lizard's
blind scurrying into weeds.
A loneliness that glided over my grandfather's
oily sweat-stained fieldworker's hat.

With red wings I hooped away
with waving arms, like a vaquero hoops
a few stray vacas back into the herd.
I twirled and skipped and hooped
every morning, for the old, dark-skinned man
who gave me a smile as he walked to work.

("As a Niño I Believed")

I generally ask the class what abstract word they suppose the poet had in mind when he wrote that poem. What emotion he felt for his grandfather as he recalled the details of his time with him. Someone usually answers, "Love." And, of course, that is what the poem is truly "about." But not once does the poet actually use that word.

This poem is from a collection of Baca's called *Martin and Meditations on the South Valley* (New Directions, 1987). It is sometimes useful to point out here to my students that Baca served time in prison and that some of his poetry deals with that subject matter in an explicit way. He was also the son of an alcoholic father, and some of his poems explore the frustrations of codependency. With many at-risk students both these topics are important yet seldom discussed in regular classes.

After we read the poem out loud, I ask the students to look at it again. Notice that he uses language that is common to his culture, that of a Chicano living in New Mexico; words like *niño, maiz, adobe, vaquero, vaca.* These words do two things: they give the poem a sense of place, and they lend an authenticity, a uniqueness, to his voice. Baca's images are clear and simple: a face like "*maiz* dough," " brown-water words," and yet, they're fresh, original.

When he does use the abstract word "loneliness," he tells you that no one could see it (as with all abstractions) but that he could *sense* it "in a horse's tail/a cow's glum dumb look…" In other words, he gives us enough particulars so that we have a clear painting of this Chicano boy's feelings. And when he twirls and skips and hoops at the end of the poem, we can feel the elation, the exhilaration, the release from the pull of the negative feelings which the child transcends, and in doing so elevates the reader, and (we suspect) the grandfather as well to whom the child's dance is a gift.

When I read this poem in class aloud, I twirl and skip at the end as well. It is a poem that lends itself to this kind of playfulness, and it is appreciated by young audiences as well as mature ones.

Here we see the clarity, simplicity, and concrete imagery derived from Baca's Mexican American background that have not only made him accessible to all ages and races, but also brought a refreshing newness to the contemporary poetry scene. Wikipedia lists him as a major American poet. But he is more. He is a universal poet for our age whose words resonate in many tongues and will echo into the future.

CHAPTER TWELVE

ARGUING WITH SEAMUS HEANEY

Seamus Heaney (1939 – 2013) was an Irish poet, translator and playwright. A recipient of the Nobel Prize, his work has become popular in many countries and has been translated into a dozen languages. Born a Catholic in Northern Ireland, he was witness to much of the violence in that region during the troubles.

When I first met Seamus Heaney in 1976, he was relatively unknown in the United States. His bio which he sent to Lois Shelton at the Poetry Center said that he was the Head of the English Department at Carysfort College in Dublin. None of the students in our MFA program had read anything by him. When I learned that he was to be one of the scheduled readers at the University, I went to the library to see if we had any of his books. We did not. I finally was able to place an order from Bookmans in Tucson and have a copy of *Wintering Out (1972)*, and his most recent book *North* (1975) shipped to me.

My fellow students and I were disappointed that some of the other readers we had asked for, such as Joyce Carol Oates, Mary Oliver, and

Naomi Shihab Nye, were not included in the annual reading series. So, as you will see, I was occasionally argumentative with Heaney.

As usual, however, I did my homework. Both my son and I read several of Heaney's poems. Those from his first book were focused on the details of the parochial, rural life in Northern Ireland. Heaney spent a great deal of time as a young man working in and around the local bogland and farms. These pieces were only mildly interesting. The second book I purchased, however, was much more compelling. Several of the poems in *North* were about bodies found preserved in the peat bogs. Besides being of anthropological and historical interest, they were also fascinating in that they seemed to touch on the Troubles in Northern Ireland and sought to place the sectarian violence there in the wider context of human experience. The following excerpt below was from a poem that both my son and I found both moving and revealing about the narrator. We could see the complexity of feelings, the sympathy, the partial rationalization, and even the faintheartedness to confront the violence which is so often the heritage of a repressed population.

> *I can feel the tug*
> *of the halter at the nape*
> *of her neck, the wind*
> *on her naked front....*
>
> *I can see her drowned*
> *body in the bog,*
> *the weighing stone,*

the floating rods and boughs....
her shaved head

like a stubble of black corn,
her blindfold a soiled bandage,
her noose a ring
to store
the memories of love.

Little adulteress....

My poor scapegoat,
I almost love you
but would have cast, I know,
the stones of silence....   *("Punishment")*

I noted as well that Heaney carefully navigated the violence, drawing a parallel with that of the present but refraining from taking any position or even asserting any moral authority. I found that a bit disturbing and intended to mention it when he came to our poetry seminar the next day or, if the opportunity presented itself, in a private conversation after the reading that evening.

****

He began the evening class by introducing himself and speaking in general terms about poetry, the importance of feeling centered in a landscape, about moving locally from the particular to the general. He spoke about his childhood in the countryside where his love of language was rooted and grew. Then he read a couple of "hearth poems" which reflected that love. One was about digging peat and how his father did it with care and purpose, and that while the poet had no shovel, he was doing something similar with a pen, digging into the past to bring sustenance to the present. After his reading and commentary, he asked if we had any questions. The silence was surprisingly extended and since there were less than a dozen of us, I thought I would begin the discussion by asking a rather simple question.

"Why do you include words in your poetry which are inaccessible to the average reader?"

"By the average reader, you mean the average American reader?" Heaney asked, smiling.

"Well, not necessarily. I mean there are some words…."

"I think T.S. Eliot said it best. Most Americans are annoyed by poems they don't immediately understand, and contemptuous of poems they understand too easily."

"Hmm. I believe it was Auden who made that comment. But if a word is obscure and interferes with the reader's appreciation or sense of the poem…"

"But, Michael, isn't it the readers responsibility to look up any words they don't understand?" one of the participants in the seminar commented, coming to Heaney's rescue

"Thank you!" Heaney said, relieved. "What is your name?

"Jonathan Millhouse."

"Quite so, Jonathan. I agree it is the reader's responsibility. Plus, I don't use words that I haven't myself heard or used in the everyday language of the country that I live in."

"But when the word is in a dialect or is unique to a particular region, say the Derry region of Ireland…" I suggested.

"Well, then it is a matter of social inclusion. That is my primary audience after all. For all those who respond to my voice and who come from that culture, it promotes a feeling of belonging, a connection, a stand against the idea of a monolingual identity compelled by British cultural imperialism."

"Much like Mexican Americans including Spanish words in their poems written in English?" Jonathan suggested.

"Exactly!"

"Fine," I answered, still unwilling to surrender my point about those few poems which had frustrated me. "But if the word is a slang term or a dialect of Spanish, like *ruca* for girlfriend instead of *novia*, or *mayate* for black person instead of *negro* for then it becomes more like *social exclusion.*"

"Well, I suppose some might feel that way, Michael, but let's move on."

Later, I would discover that regardless of Jonathan's comment about the reader's responsibility, I could not find Heaney's troublesome word choices in any standard dictionary. What was *dailigone* for instance, or *braird*? Or how about *bawn* and *rickle*? And what in the world was *hirpling*? And, despite Heaney's dismissal of my criticism, it wasn't until many years later, after Heaney had become quite famous for more inclusive work, that Maura Johnson would produce a book on Heaney's vocabulary entitled *From Aftergrass to Yellow Boots: A Glossary of Seamus Heaney's Heath Language*. This book which was published in 2021 would list and define words not only unique to South Derry but to remote rural regions at a particular time in history. These words were an amalgam of Irish and Scots dialect, Elizabethan English, and Lowland Scots. The book, which is of interest mainly to linguists and Heaney scholars, would likely not have found a publisher at all had Heaney not received the Nobel Prize.

[So the reader will not be left in the lurch as I was, here at last are the meanings: *daligone* (dawn), *braird* (first shoots of grass) hirpling (limping), *bawn* (a meadow) and *rickle* (a loosely piled heap). Thanks to the work of Maura Johnson fifty years after Heaney wrote them, they can now be found a bit more easily.]

******

But this was 1976 and Heaney was a relatively unknown and minor poet, teaching at a small college in Dublin, with few readers outside of his bailiwick. That would change especially with the publication of *North*, although I would not read the important second half of the book until later that week. The Nobel Prize was nineteen years away and the Good Friday agreement which would bring peace to Northern Ireland was twenty-three years distant. But it is not improbable that the Nobel Committee decision and the international focus on the peace agreement were related. Often the award has as much to do with the politics of the day as it does with the work of the artist. John Steinbeck's case and that of Czeslaw Milosz (who would become a great friend of Heaney's) are a couple of examples of how the two factors appear to coincide, and there are dozens of others.

I was asked by Lois Shelton if I would accompany Heaney back to the Poet's Cottage where he was staying. The route was pretty straightforward but still easy to get lost if you were unfamiliar with the campus, especially in the dark. During the walk back he commented on the number of stars that he observed in the sky. He thought it quite rare in any major city in the US, although it was still not uncommon in rural Ireland. But Dublin, he said, grows more and more each day. More traffic, more construction, and a night sky which now holds fewer and fewer stars for the naked eye.

I told him about the decision of the Tucson residents and the city council to make "dark sky" a priority and he thought it was wonderful. By the time we reached the cottage we were getting along so well, I felt comfortable accepting his invitation to join him for a "cuppa" of Irish tea. Besides, I had brought the two books of his poetry along and wanted him to sign them.

After we had settled with the tea which he had brought from Ireland because "there is no decent tea in America," he signed my copy of *Wintering Out. Poet to poet. Warmest best wishes, Seamus.*" And then picked up the copy of *North* to do the same. He paused before he wrote the second dedication and asked, "What did you think of this book?"

"I must confess, I only read the first half... but I thought it was a much finer book, and more important than your previous work. A few of the poems in *North* truly moved me. My son, Gary, I think, told you after your reading last night how much we both enjoyed "Punishment," although *enjoy* is probably not the word. A disturbing poem that made me reflect and go inward."

"Yes, well the bogs have a way of bringing forth reminders that we are not far from the terrible violence of the past, despite the trappings of modernity."

"Hmm. But I wonder, if you merely conflate the two, aren't you avoiding the central issues which are the cause of the violence. Surely, three hundred years of British occupation, the partition after the Rising, the denial of basic human rights and opportunities to the Catholics in Derry deserve a mention"

"Do you think it is the poet's job to write about those things, Michael?"

"For the Irish poet surely. I think Padraig Pearse would agree."

"Little good it did him," replied Heaney. "And I believe Yeats held a different view at the end. Do you know his poem, "The Man and the Echo" written after the 1916 slaughter? There he questioned whether his play *Cathleen Ni Houlihan* which was shown shortly before the Rising began was provocative and caused terrible bloodshed. He wrote:

I lie awake night after night
And never get the answers right.

Did that play of mine send out
Certain men the English shot?
Did words of mine put too great strain
On that woman's reeling brain?
Could my spoken words have checked
That whereby a house lay wrecked
And all seems evil until I
Sleepless would lie down and die."

Heaney agreed that the UDA (Ulster Defense Association) and other Loyalists caused many deaths, but then he saw that the Provisional IRA (Irish Republican Army) and their cohorts with their bombs and gunman had created a bloodbath as well. "Violence begets violence. Once the stage of mutual senseless destruction has been reached and spills over to the general population, taking up sides is repulsive to anyone who honors human life."

"Even when British soldiers join the Loyalists?"

"Do you know the phrase *negative capability*?"

"Yes, From John Keats, isn't it? The ability to hold in one's mind opposing ideas and accept uncertainties and doubts, without any irritable reaching after fact and reason."

"That's where I am, not only in my poetry but also in my own mind. The situation is such now that people on both sides of the issue and even those who take no side at all are the victims of violence, and all of us are being demeaned by living in fear of random shootings and bombings that can occur any time, any day. Where is justice for the Protestant women and her child who are ripped apart by an IRA bomb? Where is the justice for the Catholic girl who is shot by an Ulster Defense gunman on her way home from school?

"I do not take a side in poetry, because both sides have become repugnant to me in their depravity. As for the colonial abuses and historical causes of the conflict, while they are clear to me, they are factors for the historian to expostulate, not the poet."

He then signed his book for me: "*For Michael. Whatever you say, say nothing. Seamus.*"

We talked then of things we had in common. Our love for the Latin Mass which was now in jeopardy in most places because of Vatican II which sought to "modernize" the Church at the expense of tradition, mystery, beautiful music and universality. We had both been altar boys and both knew our Latin. It was something we missed, although you could still find a traditional Mass in a few places if you looked hard enough.

I told him about my grandfather who grew up in Cahersiveen, County Kerry, and his early faith in the Rising, the Irish one-week revolution against the British which became a reign of terror when the British used heavy artillery, destroying buildings and killing civilians in central Dublin. The subsequent British reprisals after the rebels had surrendered, the use of firing squads to murder poets and teachers, as well a beloved labor leader who, already dying from his wounds, and was nonetheless tied to a chair and shot, mobilized the world (and especially the US) to finally put pressure on the British to come to an accord.

It was late when I arrived home, well after midnight, but I stayed up reading the second half of *North*. One of the poems had as its title, Heaney's dedication, "Whatever you say, say nothing." If you Google that phrase today, it will tell you that it is "a saying of the rebel army in Northern Ireland in the Seventies reminding its members not to speak of anything significant to citizens lest it be overheard by the enemy. It was first quoted by Seamus Heaney in his classic poem."

In fact, however, it was in use long before that. It was one of the mottos of the Irish Republican Army (IRA) in the time of the Irish War of Independence. There was also an IRA poster which appeared on buildings in the late Sixties warning civilians not to report the activities of the rebels to the British army who had occupied the region, or to the Ulster paramilitary forces, because it could end in the capture and execution of you or one of your neighbors.

What Heaney did by appropriating the phase was to give it an additional meaning. Don't betray your fellow soldier (reflected in the 1935 film *The Informer*), *Don't expose your neighbor,* became in Heaney's poem, *Don't speak out at all because you might find yourself a victim of violence.* And indeed, random bombings and shootings (some due to mistaken identities and some bit of idle gossip) did cause many innocent people to be killed. Here's a bit of the poem.

> *I'm back in winter*
> *Quarters where bad news is no longer news...*

Where media men and stringers sniff and point,
Where zoom lenses, recorders and coiled leads
Litter the hotels. The times are out of joint
But I incline as much to rosary beads

As to the jottings and analyses
of politicians and newspapermen
'They're murderers.' 'Internment, understandably...'
The voice of sanity is getting hoarse.

'Religion is never mentioned here,' of course.
'You know them by their eyes,' and hold your tongue.
'One side's as bad as the other,' never worse.
Christ, it's near time that some small leak was sprung

.

Yet for all this art and sedentary trade
I am incapable. The famous

Northern reticence, the tight gag of place
And times: yes, yes. Of the 'wee six' I sing
Where to be saved you only must save face
And whatever you say, you say nothing.

In the poem we see the poet's own struggle to say something, to write some clear truth about the conflict. But he demurs and transfers his contempt to the "news" reporters who care little for the truth or causes, but only wish to exploit the violence with photos and videos which will sell newspapers and ad time on the BBC. This self-censorship, he recognizes sadly, is also (to quote Falstaff) "the better part of valor."

There was one story (among many that I heard) from relatives and friends in Ireland at the time, of a Catholic storekeeper who was murdered by an IRA gunman when it was believed that the merchant had expressed sympathy for a Protestant neighbor who had been killed earlier that week. It was said that he even attended the funeral. The last part was not true. He was loyal to the cause. But to the sectarian zealot who shot him, it made no difference.

The poem speaks of a Northern Ireland that is parochial and divided – a place of silence and fear where it is safer to keep quiet than to say the wrong thing. But contemporary readers can also find similarities to American society today, where people do not discuss politics, religion, sexuality, or race, with any frankness or openness unless they are sure ahead of time where the opinion of the listener lies. In addition to self-censorship in the publishing world, due to "cancel culture" and the risk of a career ending choice of the wrong words at the wrong time, there is also the pressure of most citizens not to accede to any truth from another country (for example, Russia's contention that NATO encirclement was needlessly provocative, and thus an impetus to the war in Ukraine), lest one be seen as naive or even traitorous.

Heaney's poetry indeed transcended his village in County Derry and has become justifiably universal. Born in Northern Ireland Heaney was in fact a citizen of the UK. But lest there be any doubt of where his sympathies truly lay, his poetic response to the editor of the *Penguin Book of Contemporary British Poetry* should resolve them once and for all. When he discovered that a selection of his poetry was to be included in this classic compendium of British verse he wrote:

> *Don't be surprised if I demur, for, be advised*
> *My passport's green.*
> *No glass of ours was ever raised*
> *To toast the Queen.*[3]

He would also turn down the offer to be Poet Laureate of the United Kingdom. He preferred to wait until the right award would come his way. In 1995 he was the fourth Irishman to be awarded the Nobel Prize for Literature joining George Bernard Shaw, Samuel Beckett, and William Butler Yeats. All of them wrote in the English language, the language of the conqueror whose vast kingdom has largely melted away.

---

[3] *The Daily Telegraph* (London), May 11, 2009.

CHAPTER THIRTEEN

FOLLOWING A RIVER WITH WILLIAM STAFFORD

William Stafford (1914-1993) was an American poet and pacifist. He was 48 years old when his first book of poetry was published, and it received the National Book Award. Known for his quiet, unassuming voice, and poignant evocative images, he went on to publish 56 volumes of poems. Poet laureate and beloved professor at Lewis and Clark College, he was also the father of Kit Stafford, poet and essayist.

I first encountered a poem of William Stafford's in a literary magazine back in 1969. It was one which has been anthologized in almost every text on American literature. The poem was "Traveling Through the Dark" and was the title piece of his first collection. I have since used it in almost every class of poetry I have taught over the past five decades.

It is a narrative poem in which the protagonist, driving at night on a dangerous and narrow mountain road located by the lip of a canyon, encounters a recently killed deer. He stops the car and realizes he needs to remove the body from the road lest an accident occur with tragic consequences, "to swerve might make more dead." As he drags the doe across the tarmac, he discovers that she is pregnant.

> *her side was warm; her fawn lay there waiting,*
> *alive, still, never to be born.*

The narrator pauses and says "I thought hard for us all, my only swerving," then he pushes the deer off the road and down into the canyon.

The poem has everything: moment, movement, originality, internal conflict, tension, and evocation of emotion. I have used this poem successfully with students at universities and in high school classes. It is deceptively accessible, yet also has resonances which continue again and again, after multiple readings of the poem. It has never failed to spark a discussion, regardless of the age of the students commenting on it.

I bought the collection and wrote a review for the college newspaper which I sent to him with a note of gratitude, not expecting a reply. A week later I received a letter thanking me and thus began a friendship that lasted until his death in 1993. When he made his debut reading at the University of Arizona, he had written to me and asked if I had any suggestions as to poems he might share. I did and gave him a list. And I also included a poem of his that he didn't have, which had appeared in one of the many obscure journals published in the late Sixties and Seventies. At his reading he mentions this to the audience.

"And now I come to a section of the reading suggested to me by a person I know by correspondence, Michael Hogan. Some of the poems he suggested I have already included in my reading, that just happened. Others will read now, including one which I did not have that he took the trouble to send me. It is not in any book. It first appeared in the Hampden-Sydney Poetry Review, entitled "Accepting Surprise." [4]

Here is an excerpt from that poem.

The right mistakes, the rich moment when the rain finds you
A pinch from a branch in a hedge that tells you, you're real...
Mistakes like jewels...
The hidden rush and loss of a world
that throbs beyond control, good, good, never quite ours.

The next poem was a powerfully evocative one about the death of a local librarian. It was called simply "Bess." It began: "These are the streets where Bess first met her cancer." It describes how she went to work each day, "past our secure houses, while the great national events danced their grotesque, fake importance."

In the last year of her life
She had to keep her friends from knowing how happy they
were.
She listened while they complained about the food, the
weather...

---

[4] https://voca.arizona.edu/reading/william-stafford-december-1-1976

Always pain moved where she moved, she walked ahead, it
followed....

But she remembered where joy used to live,
she straightened its flowers, and when students asked for books
her hand went out to help.
...and when finally she pulled into a tiny corner
and slipped from pain, her hands open again, and the streets
opened
and she wished all well.

The audience was stunned, quiet. Then Stafford spoke again. "I don't know if you feel..." Everyone broke into a warm applause. The audience was quite moved.

"Thank you. I was going to say that I didn't know if you felt this had a place at a poetry reading." Stafford had felt it was risky to read it to an academic audience since it was very local, personal, and on the edge of the sentimental. But the audience, both young and old alike, assured him it indeed had a place.

I introduced myself after the reading, and we spontaneously hugged. He thanked me later for suggesting that poem. "I was truly touched by the reaction of the audience," he said. "I never would have guessed at the depth of their emotional response." But that was Tucson, both the locals and the university folks. It was what attracted so many poets to come there and read.

We talked briefly and then he was overwhelmed with well-wishers and people wanting copies of their books signed. I departed, knowing I would see him several more times before he left town since I was often the university go-to person for local transport, for airport pickups and departures, and sometimes dinners.

The next day he taught an undergraduate class and during the interchange with the students, one commented that he had been told by his instructor that each word in a poem was important.

"Do you agree, Mr. Stafford?" the student asked.

"No, not really," Stafford replied much to the young instructor's chagrin. Then he smiled at the instructor, a grad school teaching assistant, and said, "I believe that every syllable is important!"

Then we went on to discuss diction, use of meter, and other techniques, speaking not as a writing teacher but as a professor of literature, which was the vocation that he had dedicated his life to.

Later, as we walked back to the Poet's Cottage, we talked about how we both came to write poetry late in life, he in his forties, I in my thirties.

"I always loved poetry, Michael, much as you do, and I also had a childhood mild enough for me to pay attention to the natural world, the wood, the creek, the open fields." He spoke about the importance of focusing and shared a poem with me called "Message from the Wanderer." The relative portion was this.

> *Thus freedom always came nibbling my thought,*
> *just as—often, in light, on the open hills—*

> *you can pass an antelope and not know*
> *and look back, and then—even before you see—*
> *there is something wrong about the grass.*
> *And then you see.*

> *That is the way everything in the world is waiting.*

It was another Stafford poem I memorized, and which stayed with me both as a touchstone and as a teaching tool. You can hear three different levels of experience operating here. First is the experience we have all had walking in the woods and not seeing a deer or antelope or other creature who is right beside us and then by some trick of light or movement of the wind, suddenly discovering it is brilliantly there.

The second level is uniting that experience to freedom, which has nothing to do with free markets, the Free World or free trade, but is rather the discretionary power one has to envision the world. Stafford's father gave him permission to do that. The final line, "That's the way everything in the world is waiting," connects both of the foregoing. We have the freedom to define our life, our story, our sculpture and we need to recognize that this is a power which is not absolute or unconditional. One of the conditions is that we must purify our vision, for the awareness comes, as Stafford writes, only "in light, on the open hills." Stafford shared a narrative which went along with the poem. He said that when he was a young boy, about ten or eleven, his father and he were tramping in the woods looking for game. His father said, "Keep sharp eye peeled, Bill. You can see things better than I can."

Stafford was delighted. His father, a veteran woodsman, had told the young Stafford that the boy had superior vision. Or perhaps he meant closer powers of observation. What a gift! It gave the youthful Stafford permission to be a see-er, an observer, one with a competency which was superior to even that of his father.

Later, when he had become older, Stafford realized that perhaps all his father meant was his own eyes were failing with age. But that was unimportant. The emotional and spiritual effect on the young ten-year-old had a lifelong impact. Stafford assumed the mantle of careful observer or seer, of a visionary with all the existential power this could carry for him as a poet. His father, whether inadvertently or not, had given him permission to speak, permission to report his unique vision of the world to future generations.

To me that is such a powerful moment. What makes it powerful of course is the boy's recognition of its importance, or at least his assigning it importance. And it makes no difference what the father's intent was. For whether the moment was a teaching one or the son's interpretation was value-added, the result was the same. That moment freed the young boy to see clearly and uniquely what previously had been seen and talked about only by others.

A year later, Unicorn Press brought out a second, hardcover edition of my early book, *Letters for My Son*, and Stafford wrote a lovely back cover blurb for that edition. No doubt due to his *imprimatur*, several of the poems would soon appear in anthologies and even in a few college textbooks, including Laurence Perrine's *Sound and Sense*.

We were to meet several more times both in Arizona and a final time in Colorado. The last time I was teaching in Denver and also drinking a bit too much, probably suffering from mid-stage alcoholism, but I didn't know it at the time. I just thought I was enjoying life. I hung around with some poets who were also heavy drinkers, Jess Graf, Frank Winters, Charles Bukowski when he was in town, and the Vietnam vet, Tom Valle.

On one occasion, the four of us read some poems from a flatbed truck in Commerce City with the Devil's Disciples motorcycle club illuminating the "stage" with their headlights. Afterward we all got pretty loaded on beer, wine, and pot, while Bukowski regaled us with his theories about classical music, trivia, and the Truth, with a capital T.

"Music," he said, "is the only thing close to poetry. It is poetry in a more refined language. Everything else, including politics, careerism, and competition is just trivia. Everyone thinks that those things are important. Getting ahead, building the portfolio, the bank account, acquiring more and more. Power or influence, or wealth…as if life goes on forever with us as the center.

"But here's the Truth. We're all going to die, all of us, what a circus! That alone should make us love each other but it doesn't. We are terrorized and flattened by trivialities; we are eaten up by nothing. The only thing we really have are those transcendental moments that we can sometimes capture in words, sometimes in love, but never when we are trying to entice them. Only when we are open to them, but busy working, do they come as gifts from an unexpected and unknown source.

"Trying to entice them is what so many of these college writing programs are all about. Most who come out of that mold are vanilla extracts. Maybe not you, Hogan. But that has yet to be seen; you appear to have some street creds. And there are a few others who are okay. Etheridge Knight in Detroit, Jimmy Santiago Baca in Albuquerque, Gerald Locklin in Long Beach, Jaime Sabines down in Mexico. I don't care much for the academic poets in America but there are exceptions there, too."

"William Stafford is certainly one," Tom Valle remarked. "That dude has soul." Bukowski and I both agreed. Frank Winters was deep in his cups and made no reply. The rest of the evening passed without any memorable conversation that I can recall. By that time I was a bit lost in my own cups as well.

A few days later, Tom saw an announcement that Stafford would be reading at Northern Colorado University.

****

Thomas Valle (1947-2020) was a combat Marine with tours in Viet Nam, and the author of three books, Unsung Hero, Collected Poems of Thomas G. Valle and Blood Love and Semper Fi. According to his bio from the Colorado Poets Center: Valle was educated at the University of Denver but studied his craft under Michael Hogan, Jess Graf, Douglas Anderson, and Frank Winters. Valle was the featured poet at CSU-

Pueblo, University of Denver, and numerous coffeehouses in the Denver metro area and Boulder, for over twenty-five years.

What's not mentioned in Tom's bio, was the fact that he was also a Purple Heart veteran and had suffered from severe injuries and still had painful shrapnel lodged in his skull. He was subject to severe headaches and used alcohol and sometimes narcotics to relieve the pain. He was a survivor and never complained. But he was also sometimes erratic in his behavior and spontaneous as a child in his enthusiasms.

One of the legions of Veterans Against the War, Tom had been quite active in his protests after his return to the States, even traveling to Washington, DC to join a march there. When I told him that Stafford was a pacifist who spent six years in federal custody digging ditches, he was convinced that we had to travel up north to pay homage. So, off we went to the peaceful, quiet, and rather conservative, farming community of Greeley, Colorado.

The drive was uneventful. We played music on a tape deck, songs by Willie Nelson, Merle Haggard, Creedence Clearwater Revival. Neither of us felt that Bach or Mozart was an appropriate prelude to Greeley. We shared a couple of joints, Tom sipped at a few beers that he brought along. We arrived a couple of hours before the reading. Went to a bar that served sandwiches and I ordered a hamburger and a beer. Tom skipped on the food and ordered a beer and a shot chaser. Then, another and another. He was buying, so I thought it only polite that I match him drink for drink when I finished my hamburger. By the time we left the bar two hours later to head over to the campus we both had a bit of a buzz.

"This town smells like a damn farm," Tom commented. And, true enough, there was a strong odor of manure and fertilizer as we got closer to the college. It was in fact a university that had been founded as an agricultural institute and still had that discipline as a major. "Probably everyone in this town likes guns, short haircuts, and hates Mexicans and Indians."

Now that comment did not bode well for Tom's behavior in company. Nervously, I said, "Tom, you just got here. Give it a break."

"Why do you think they named it Greeley?" he said. "After Horace Greeley who said, 'Go West, young man, go West.' He didn't give a damn that half of the West was Mexican Territory, and the other half was populated by Indians. The US Army would conquer the first and run the Mexicans off, then slaughter most of the second, and herd the survivors onto reservations. *Manifest Destiny,* they called it. No need to prove it. It was America's destiny, God's will, to take over the entire continent from sea to shining sea! Manifest means it's obvious what God intended, no need to prove it was right. Just do it."

The reading was held in the Michener Library (named after the novelist who was a Colorado native) and there was a group of about forty to fifty in attendance. A much smaller turnout than the University of Arizona readings where there were often 300 or more. In addition, the audience was almost exclusively white, with men dressed in sports coats and women in skirts and blouses. There were very few locals in the group.

After a brief introduction, Stafford did his thing. Although it was a respectful audience, most of the poems drew only light applause. We were more than halfway through, and Tom was nodding off, the effect of the booze and pot taking effect. Then Stafford read "At the Bomb Testing Site." It was not an obvious protest poem. The lead character in the poem was a small, silent lizard as it sits somewhat tense in a huge expanse of desert. There is no moral judgment, all the reader is given is the certainty of violent change under the indifferent sky. But for some reason (Instinct? Hearing the word bomb in the title?) Tom was now wide awake. The next poem, though still in Stafford's gentle voice and understatement, was more direct. In the relevant portion, it went

> *This town is haunted by some good deed*
> *that reappears like a country cousin, or truth*
> *when language falters these days trying to lie...*
>
> *Our Senator talked like war, and Aunt Mabel*
> *said, "He's a brilliant man,*
> *but we didn't elect him that much."*
>
> *Everyone's resolve weakens toward evening*
> *or in a flash when a face melds...:*
> *There are Aunt Mabels all over the world,*
> *or their graves in the rain.*

"OOH-RAH!" yelled Tom, now wide awake and applauding heartily. He whistled and shouted again, OOH-RAH. ABSOLUTELY! Then turned to me in a loud voice: "*We didn't elect him that much.* Don't you love it?"

A handful of students and a couple of professors applauded, and I cheered enthusiastically along with Tom, not willing to abandon a friend. But the majority of the audience was not only silent but frowning and clearly displeased. I looked over at the faculty chair who had introduced Stafford earlier, and he was glaring in our direction, clearly angry. Stafford read a few more poems, including his hallmark poem, "A Ritual to Read to Each Other" and then sat down to polite applause (except for Tom who showed his approval by an enthusiastic "Bravo!" and a whistle or two).

The chairman then announced that "There will be a reception for Dr. Stafford at the Oak Room at Crabbe Hall with wine and cheese. Faculty members and special guests of Dr. Stafford at the university are cordially invited to attend."

When Tom and I arrived at the Oak Room we were met at the door by the chairman who blocked our way.

"I'm sorry, gentlemen, but this event is reserved for faculty and friends."

"What the hell!" said Tom. "Mike, tell this guy something…"

I was about to apologize for our enthusiasm at the reading but, before I could say a word, Stafford appeared in the doorway.

"Ah, Michael. So good to see you! Thanks so much for coming all this way." Then to the director, "This is Professor Michael Hogan and his colleague. Dr. Hogan is a good friend of mine from the University of Arizona."

It was typical of Stafford's grace and his loyalty. He embraced Tom and me with an open heart. That was his grace. As far as loyalty went, it had been part of his life for the longest time, sticking with quiet courage to his pacifism and love of country, amid unspeakable abuse during the War. Also, remaining a professor with a meager salary at a small liberal arts college in Oregon when, as a famous author, he was offered positions at prestigious universities at twice that amount.

The poem with which he ended his reading is worth mentioning again here. It is one that I have read to every class that I have taught over the years. It is sometimes mere bold statement, without metaphor or music. And yet, despite its straightforwardness and simplicity, it reverberates in the heart. It is called a "Ritual to Read to Each Other":

If you don't know the kind of person I am
and I don't know the kind of person you are
a pattern that others made may prevail in the world...

For there is many a small betrayal in the mind,
a shrug that lets the fragile sequence break...

And so I appeal to a voice, to something shadowy,
a remote important region in all who talk:
though we could fool each other, we should consider—
lest the parade of our mutual life get lost in the dark.
For it is important that awake people be awake,

or a breaking line may discourage them back to sleep;
the signals we give – yes or no, or maybe—
should be clear: the darkness around us is deep.

You know a poem has become part of the culture when you hear it quoted, or a line becomes a commonplace allusion. My wife, when I misspeak, or tell a white lie, will often say to me, *Be careful, Michael. The darkness around us is deep.* In our kitchen in Mexico is a framed broadside of a Stafford poem, produced by Ryan Petty of Cold Mountain Press in Austin, Texas. It was given to me that night in Greeley, Colorado, and has graced our various homes for the past forty years. The poem is "Love the Earth Like a Mole" and the inscription reads, *To Michael Hogan and Family with respect and admiration. Bill Stafford. April 1980.*

In 1993 while teaching at the American School of Guadalajara, I announced to my AP Literature class that William Stafford had died. One of the students wondered if it would be okay to translate "A Ritual to Read to Each Other" into Spanish. I thought that was a great idea. He did a fine job, and we sent a copy to Stafford's wife Dorothy. The last line graces my office at the school today where I continue to write poems and mentor students, as emeritus head of humanities:

Las señales que damos—sí o no, o tal vez—
deben quedar claro: la oscuridad que nos rodea es profunda.

CHAPTER FOURTEEN

TO BE ONE'S BEST SELF WITH NAOMI SHIHAB NYE

Naomi Shihab Nye (1952-) is an American poet, editor, novelist, and songwriter. Born of an American mother and a Palestinian father, she is multicultural both in her approach to literature and her appeal to readers worldwide. Author of more than forty books, and editor of several anthologies, she has received numerous awards for her work including the prestigious Guggenheim Fellowship. An alumna of Trinity College in San Antonio where she makes her home, she is "permanent professor of writing" at Texas State University. Much appreciated by teachers and students alike for her openness and accessibility, she was the Poetry Foundation's Young People Laureat in 2021 and has been active with the writers in the schools' program for many years.

I once asked William Stafford if he would recommend a contemporary poet I should read. He was reluctant. "I don't like to do that," he said. As a literature teacher his focus was always on poets prior to T.S. Eliot and the moderns. He said there were several contemporaries that he enjoyed but said that he didn't want to influence my reading or "dilute" my own discoveries. "However, I will say this. If you run across a book of poems by Naomi Shihab Nye, you might pick it up. Her poems will reward the time you spend with them. She writes things that I sometimes wish I had written. They are poems of ordinary life but somehow filled with grace-notes that echo."

I did not take him up on it at the time but in 1986 I saw that she was scheduled to read at the University Arizona, so I picked up two books of her poems ahead of time. They accompanied me across three continents, battered and stained from the elements and spilled coffee.

Her reading venue was packed with university folks as well as townsfolks and she was a compelling presence on the stage. Poised, thoughtful, open, and totally sincere. She told a story of when she and her newlywed husband were on their honeymoon in South America, traveling from one end of the continent to the other by bus. It was an adventure that soon turned into a nightmare. She told how they were robbed and how she was devastated and frightened. By the side of the road in a foreign country with no money, no passport, and no food. She talked about the kindness of strangers who stopped to help and then she read a poem called "Kindness."

> *Before you know what kindness really is*
> *you must lose things,*
> *feel the future dissolve in a moment*
> *like salt in a weakened broth....*

She then describes the crowded bus with its rooftop baggage and live chickens that will go on to the next village. We observe the dead Indio by the side of the road. She evokes feelings of fear, desolation, panic, that one feels having been robbed, or lost in a strange country. But these feelings also have echoes in our own moments of grief, of loneliness, of sorrow. We feel that we are alone and there is no help for us. That the past is irredeemable and the present uncertain and perilous. It is then that the kind words of a stranger can save us.

But if this was all the poem was "about" it would not be a poem of Nye's. For she always hints at a moral obligation that tragic experience demands of us, much like William James described in his *Varieties of Religious Experience*. Our sorrows and grief should remind us of the importance of our kindness to others. That is the moral imperative she hints at.

> *Before you know kindness as the deepest thing inside,*
> *you must know sorrow as the other deepest thing.*
> *You must wake up with sorrow.*
> *You must speak to it till your voice*
> *catches the thread of all sorrows*
> *and you see the size of the cloth.*

In the end that is the only true value of suffering, of loss, of grief. Not some stoic victory lap on social media: "I survived cancer" or the Nietzschean "Whatever does not destroy me makes me stronger." Rather, the discovery that

...it is only kindness that makes sense anymore,
only kindness that ties your shoes
and sends you out into the day to gaze at bread,
only kindness that raises its head
from the crowd of the world to say
It is I you have been looking for,
and then goes with you everywhere
like a shadow or a friend.

There is an intimacy between Nye and the audience that I have witnessed with only a couple of other poets in my lifetime, and then only for the period of a poem or two. Nye seems to hold this intimacy for a much longer time, in fact it echoes with some long after she has left the stage.

Susan North, a well-known Tucson poet and teacher, told me that she has several Nye poems posted with magnets on her fridge, a reminder of how the commonplace can bring beauty to the kitchen and make the day feel special.

As a poet and as a person, what I most love about Nye is her humility, a quality rare in so many artists, let alone one of her extraordinary success and public acclaim. Humility, it is said, is not thinking less of yourself, but thinking of yourself less. In her wonderful poem "Famous," she writes:

I want to be famous to shuffling men
who smile while crossing streets,

sticky children in grocery lines,
famous as the one who smiled back.

I want to be famous in the way a pulley is famous,
or a buttonhole, not because it did anything spectacular,
but because it never forgot what it could do.

I realize I am straying far from any analytic or academic analysis of her work. But I do not apologize for the digression. As a teacher for over forty years, I find that when I bring her work to one of my literature or creative writing cases, the students come alive, they share their own stories, they speak of empathy, they speak of the loss of civility in society and what they can do to remedy it. Nye is never dogmatic, never pontificates. Her poetry is not didactic. But the suggestions in the poem, sometimes the poet's own searching within, call to the reader in ways that are truly powerful.

During her Tucson visit, I almost missed her. Although I stood in line waiting for my books to be signed, I despaired because of the length of the line and went to get a quick drink at a bar close by. When I returned, she was packing up and getting ready to leave. But I did manage to tag along with Richard and Lois Shelton, and Steve and Gail Orlen, who had invited her to have some Mexican food at a restaurant called The Neighborhood. The place was small and crowded but we managed to find seats, enjoyed some of the best Mexican food in the Southwest and talked about poetry. I told her about Stafford's recommendation, and she smiled shyly and said that he was her mentor and that she did not go a day without feeling grateful for his presence in her life. I told her that the same was true for me as well.

In the months that followed, my heavy drinking turned into a compulsion. I went to San Francisco, where I eventually crashed and burned, and lived through some desolate and hopeless months. Then, through some timely intercessions, I recovered, picked myself up, got a job locally and then one in Mexico where I have served as a teacher and department chair for three decades.

In 1990, William Stafford died, later I suffered family losses as well. Naomi wrote me a letter not long afterwards asking if I would be interested in submitting some poems for an anthology she was editing. Her letter sat on my desk unanswered for months, until one day it disappeared, blown by the wind, who knows? Overwhelmed by losses in my own family, I was barely holding myself together and not corresponding with anyone. But I did have the poems, the stories.

I remembered recently reading an interview with Kim Stafford and Naomi Shihab Nye in which Kim spoke of his father's last days and the conversations they had. He said that he remembered his dad telling the story of when he was a young boy of eleven or twelve sitting at the kitchen table at the family home in Kansas reading. Suddenly there was a loud bang. When he ran to the door to see what happened he found his dog, Buster, who had been struck by a car on the highway, struggling to get up on the front porch, clearly dying, but safe home. His father's eyes filled with tears. "My dad did not cry easily." Kim recalled. He said that he looked around as if there was someone who could help but there was no one. He was alone in the darkness as the dog died under his loving hands.

Naomi and Kim both referenced then the poem "Traveling Through the Dark" and how the narrator finds a dead deer on the highway, but pregnant with a "never to be born" calf. Now Stafford has his narrator (perhaps the poet himself?) alone as an adult, facing a terrible decision. "To swerve would make more dead." So, the narrator pauses (I thought hard for us all "my only swerving") before doing what he has to do, pushing dead deer into the canyon. "That is such a great line!" Naomi said. "'I thought hard for us all.' How we are all alone when we make those kinds of difficult decisions yet, we are not totally alone. There are those other voices."

How we work our way through our griefs and our sorrow, how they inform our lives as artists, as workers, as caregivers, these are important decisions. They are not strategies or solutions that poetry teaches so much as they are opportunities for us to visualize and teach ourselves.

Reading her work, I experience again the possibility of the healing that can be found in poetry; how it can rescue us even though we are distant both in time and geography from those who wrote the words. Bill Stafford was dead; Naomi I hadn't seen in twenty years or more. And yet there were the poems. As she once reminded all of us:

> *When your hope shrinks*
> *you might feel the hope of*
> *someone far away lifting you up.*

Hope is the thing ...
Hope was always the thing!
What else did we give each other
from such distances?
Breath of syllables,
sing to me from your balcony
please! Befriend me
in the deep space.
When you pause for a poem
it could reshape the day
you had just been living. ("Every day as a wide field, every
page")

And so it was, and so it is today. She continues to encourage us to become our best selves.

CHAPTER FIFTEEN

DAYS OF WINE AND ROSES WITH RICHARD HUGO AND TESS GALLAGHER

Despite Ernest Dowson's assurance that "they are not long, the days of wine and roses," they do appear so at the time. For me, alcohol and later drugs enhanced my perceptions, propelled my writing, released my inhibitions, and made me a colorful performer and lecturer. I enjoyed life, and those around me found me to be an entertaining companion. There were glitches, however. There was the occasional binge and late-night partying that resulted in a debilitating hangover the next day. Then there were times when I did not recall certain things that I had done or said the night before.

Looking back, I can see there were warning signs. I received a note on an essay in literary criticism that I had written for Francine Prose, the famed novelist who was a visiting professor, which read, "Michael, this is not Honors work!" Her grade was a C. In the MFA program, two grades of C meant loss of the fellowship. So, I cleaned up and completed the course with a B+ and obtained the degree. Whew! Then, when I was being considered for an assistantship, I went to a party where I apparently insulted the Dean of Liberal Arts. The poet Tess Gallagher rather sternly suggested that I go to a campus AA meeting. I did so, and then went out for coffee with some of the other grad students and professors after the meeting but all they talked about was drinking and recovery. I was annoyed. "Come on," I said. "After a whole hour of AA, can't we talk about something else." I just didn't get it.

After receiving my MFA, there were many missed opportunities due to my drinking. I was offered a contract to ghost write the biography of one of the Beach Boys. But I failed to meet the deadline with the initial chapters, after several unanswered requests, the contract was canceled. I was offered a two-page spot in the *New York Times Book Review* to write a review of Thomas Merton's latest book, and failed to deliver, essentially ensuring that I was blacklisted by that magazine. The writing wasn't working for me, and teaching opportunities were lost as well. I missed a temporary teaching gig at a university in California because I got drunk in the airport and never made it to the interview. My behavior became more and more self-destructive.

My wife, Jojo Daneker, divorced me in Colorado just after my daughter's second birthday party to which I arrived late, after an afternoon of drinking. Determined to change my life, I moved back to Arizona where I did legal research for the prominent criminal law attorney, Stanford Bloom. My son was still living with me but now, at age 18 he decided to move back with his mother in Colorado. I made decent money as a legal researcher and was offered a more permanent job with Southwest Legal Services. After several three-day benders, including one in which I flew to Boston to see the Red Sox in the playoffs and then passed out in the MTA subway and ended up in a drunk tank, I was told that my services were no longer needed at the Tucson law offices. So, I came to believe that Arizona was the problem and felt that if I moved to a more liberal location, my luck would change.

So, I moved to California, where I proceeded inexplicably to go through the rest of my savings and ended up bumming handouts from contacts and friends. Sleeping on Arthur Ferlinghetti's couch one night at City Lights' Books, then in the wooded hills above San Francisco Bay for more than a week. I remembered the poem by Edward Arlington Robinson, about Mister Flood, another remorseful alcoholic:

> *He raised again the jug regretfully*
> *And shook his head and was again alone.*
> *There was not much that was ahead of him,*
> *And there was nothing in the town below—*
> *Where strangers would have shut the many doors*
> *That many friends had opened long ago. ("Mister Flood's*
> *Party")*

My life was a mess. I contemplated suicide as I sipped from the last bottle of wine bought with the small loan Ferlinghetti advanced me. After a few nights in the cold damp of the woods, I had developed a persistent cough, then bronchitis. I got up the last morning that I can remember from this episode and headed toward downtown. It had been days since I had eaten any solid food. Somewhere on Market Street I collapsed and woke up in the emergency room of San Francisco General Hospital. I was told that I was suffering from malnutrition and pleural pneumonia and was on the edge of death. The pneumonia was so advanced that to save my life they needed to make an incision in my back, insert a tube, and drain the fluid from my lungs. Because of my alcoholism and drug use the doctor said he could not give me a sedative. He asked me if I wanted the chaplain to be with me. I told him I really didn't care.

So, the chaplain came and recited the Lord's Prayer over and over as the doctor performed the operation. It was successful and I began a slow recovery with oxygen, intravenous antibiotics, and an enriched diet. When it came time for my discharge, Dr. Clint Potter, the attending physician, told me he was reluctant to let me go back to the streets. He was certain that I would die. But there were no openings in the Alcohol and Drug Rehabilitation Center, and in the hospital itself, all the beds were full. But there was one possibility. Would I be willing to work outside the hospital emergency room from 2 am until 6 am, every day, meeting the ambulances and hosing down the gurneys after they delivered the victims of accidents? If so, it would ensure me a cot in the corridor each evening, and my meals. During the day I would go to AA meetings.

There followed a month of rude awakenings. Hosing down gurneys covered with blood and gore, I witnessed victims of stabbings, shootings, and domestic violence. I saw self-inflicted gunshot wounds, and drug overdoses. I saw bodies ripped apart in automobile accidents.

One after another I heard from first responders that the vast majority of these tragedies were the result of drug or alcohol abuse. Seeing a four-year-old girl whose skull was shattered when a car driven by her drunken mother hit a telephone pole, was enough of a reminder that the addict affects not only himself or herself but all who are touched by their behavior: children, spouses, friends, and innocent drivers with whom they cross paths. It is said that the life of an alcoholic or addict negatively affects the lives of twenty others. I believe that is a very low estimate.

I was off the booze and drugs, chastised and humbled. And, although some days uncomfortable in my own skin, I was nonetheless grateful for the reprieve from compulsive behavior. I began doing community service, attending recovery meetings, and finally was offered a job teaching at-risk students which I accepted enthusiastically. My life had changed dramatically. And there were many blessings, including meeting my present wife of thirty-four years. But frustratingly, the thing I treasured most, did not return as quickly as I hoped. All my attempts at writing, whether poetry or prose, were pitiful, banal, and unimaginative. It was as if the alcohol spirits had killed *the* Spirit which had gifted me with words and inspired me in the past. I knew other poets who had undergone this change from alcoholic drinking to recovery, I wondered if one of them might help. I decided to write to a poet whose early work I had reviewed and whom I knew has his own struggles with addiction.

****

The Rocky Road to Recovery

Richard Hugo (1923-1982) was an American poet best known for his work rooted in the Pacific Northwest but whose depth and impact extended far beyond mere regionalism. Like Theodore Roethke who was his mentor, Hugo plumbed the depths of his own consciousness with his struggles against addiction, despair, and the grinding isolation of cities to mold a poetry that was universal. The author of sixteen books of poetry, he was a voice of hope and resilience.

Three days later I received a call. "Hello, Mike. This is Dick Hugo. I read your letter and would be glad to help. How long have you been off the sauce?" he asked. I told him only a few months. "Then I presume you have not done an inventory and shared it with another person. You haven't made amends to those you hurt by your drinking and using. Am I right?" I told him that he was. He then asked if I had a sponsor, I told him I did, but hadn't really talked with him much.

"Well, here's your problem with writing. You must have a free mind to create. And right now, your mind is cluttered up with regrets for the things you did or didn't do when you were drinking and using. It is also cluttered with resentments against those who you think did you wrong. And you're worried about the future and how you're going to make a living, right? Unless you can get rid of those regrets, resentments and fears, your mind will not be free to create. You'll never write another decent poem. The words will be fake."

"So, what do I do? How can I begin?"

"Get with your sponsor. He'll help you list all of your regrets, fears, and resentments. It's called an inventory. When it is all written down, share it with him, or another person, it could even be me if you wish. After that, you begin by making amends to those you have hurt."

"I can see that this is important, but I don't see how it is going to help my writing."

"Let me give you a metaphor, Mike. You have braided a noose during your drinking composed of fuckups, missed appointments and deadlines, lost jobs, family abuse, insults to others, unpaid debts and God knows what other trash. That noose is choking off the life force; the spirit from which your poetry comes. You blame yourself for some of it, this causes remorse, regret, *if only* kind of thinking. You also blame others for some of your failures. Thus, you have resentments as well. Now without a job, and having burnt so many bridges, you are fearful about the future. You need to deal with that, to be free from that before you can write. Right now, you have one leg in the past and the other in the future, and you are pissing on the present.

"Do you know the James Wright poem 'In a Hammock at Duffy's Farm?'"

I did not, so he recited a few lines that he knew out loud.

> "*Over my head, I see the bronze butterfly,*
> *Asleep on the black trunk*
> *Blowing like a leaf in green shadow.*
> *Down the ravine behind the empty house...*

To my right,
In a field of sunlight between two pines...
I lean back, as the evening darkens and comes on.
A chicken hawk floats over, looking for home
I have wasted my life."

"I'm not sure I understand it," I told him.

"Well, like any poem it can mean different things to different readers. But to the recovering alcoholic? Think about it. He is in a hammock at Duffy's Farm recovering from another bout of hopeless drunkenness after he had sworn to quit. Now as he lies there, he has a blessed moment where he is completely focused on the external world: the butterflies, the ravine, the chicken hawk. He is not thinking about himself, his worries, his regrets, his resentments. In that moment of self-forgetfulness, he realizes that the ego and its compulsion have blocked him from the appreciation, the wonder, of daily life and its miracles. That is what has happened to you as well. You had it once and lost it. It was a gift, and you threw it away. That's the wasted part. And it will continue until you do the work of unraveling the rope of the past that binds you. Take an inventory, clean house, share it with another alcoholic, make amends, and you will see the change."

I took his advice and also consulted with Dr. Clint Potter, the emergency resident who had saved me. He replied, "Well, everything your friend told you is true. But what is also true is that you have killed thousands of brain cells by your drinking. And they do not grow back. But the good news is that you can create new pathways, new synapses, and make inactive cells functional. After all, we only use a small portion of the brain. So, start keeping a journal, do some community service. Write about others that you work with. Give the brain some food to grow."

Shortly thereafter, I had a note from Dick Hugo. He wrote in part:

"Don't give up; it will happen, and when it does you will be amazed. When I finished making amends and really getting sober, it was almost like poems had piled up in me, and I just started writing and writing and writing… I mean I was really getting a kick, just discovering ways to move and things to say, which is a lot of the fun of writing, surprising yourself on the page. Right now, you are dry, which is a bit different from being sober. It will come, my friend, it will come. But don't force it. Above all, don't write about anything that needs a poem written about it!

"By the way, did you know we might be cousins? My father, Richard Franklin Hogan, left us just after my mom gave birth. I was raised by my mom's parents and had my name changed to Hugo when I was eighteen. I had a resentment about him as well, but I dealt with it. Now I know that my father did what he had to do to save himself, and I forgave him long ago.

****

Tess Gallagher (b. 1943—) is an American poet, essayist, and short story writer. Her work has appeared in a myriad of periodicals, literary journals, and anthologies. She is the author of twenty books, and recipient of both the NEA and the Guggenheim fellowships. She divides her time between Port Angeles, Washington, and Ballidoon, Co. Sligo, Ireland.

It had been ten years since Tess Gallagher and I were on the University of Arizona campus together. She and Lois Shelton had teamed up on me after an evening when I had insulted the Dean of Liberal Arts and jeopardized any chance of a university job. They both suggested that I go to an AA meeting and work on my sobriety. I did so, but it didn't stick. In addition, I harbored a silent resentment over their interference which persisted for many years. I didn't know then that they both had experience with alcoholism in their families and knew a bit about the disease. Tess would marry Ray Carver right around that time. He was a recovering alcoholic himself, but she never knew him during his drinking days. Nevertheless, she learned more and more about recovery in their decade of living together and had become a quiet voice for recovery programs.

Tess is a fine poet, and I was pleased to have an opportunity to meet with her again and let go of my resentment. I had some time to reflect on the fact that if I changed the way I looked at things, the things I looked at changed as well. In light of what I had learned, Tess's intervention now made perfect sense. But the great thing was now I was sober, and we would meet again. The occasion, however, was a somber one. It was 1989 and Ray Carver had died the year before of brain cancer. So, Tess's reading was not so much of her own work, but rather presenting a posthumous collection of poetry, journal entries and other pieces by Ray Carver entitled, *A New Path to the Waterfall* for which she had written the introduction.

I took a ferry with my sponsor, Bill Hicks, from San Francisco to Larkspur. The location of the reading was the College of Marin in San Rafael in a lovely theater. Tess wore a red suit and matching shoes. Her dark hair flowed unimpeded down her back and shone in the stage spotlight with gold highlights. She was a commanding presence, sure of herself, with an inner beauty that lit up when she smiled. As my mother would say, "She had the map of Ireland on her face."

She spoke a bit about Ray Carver and their relationship during his final decade of life. She read several of his poems, including the now famous, "Gravy," which has since been published in the *New Yorker* and anthologized in dozens of texts. It is a powerful piece about recovery and gratitude. She talked about good intentioned friends who suggested that after a year of mourning, it was time that she moved on and formed a new relationship. She smiled sadly and said what even her best friends did not understand was that when you had the perfect love, anything that followed would be a disappointment and unfair to anyone you inflicted it on. It was a moving presentation and several in the audience (including Bill and I were moved to tears). Bill commented, "I don't know much about poetry, but I do know about people. Tess Gallagher is the real deal."

Tess didn't read any of her own poems or stories, much to my disappointment. But I understood. This was both a requiem for a creative presence which had passed from the world, and a tribute to love.

We bought Carver's posthumous book and Tess graciously wrote a dedication on her introduction page. When the crowds left, we went out for coffee together. We spoke of many things, but recovery was on both our minds, and how we rescue one another, and what the future might hold. She intended to go to Ireland, perhaps even buy a home and settle there. It was where her roots were and her family's history.

For me, the future was still uncertain. I told her about my part-time teaching gig, my only source of income. Money from poetry readings and public appearances had dried up, mostly because of cutbacks in funding since the Reagan days. State universities and community colleges no longer had budgets supplemented by state education funds. Their coffers had been decimated due to tax breaks for corporations and the wealthy. The NEA stopped funding the hundreds of once-flourishing literary magazines due to budget cuts.

"You should consider writing articles on creative writing, or history, or even a memoir. I make ten times more income from prose, especially nonfiction articles than I ever made from either poetry or short stories. You might also think about going abroad. Poets are far more honored abroad these days, than they are in America. Maybe Ireland, or even Mexico?"

I would end up following her advice in both instances. Lucinda and I moved to Mexico the following year and never looked back. I was appointed Head of English at a prestigious private school, obtained a PhD in Latin American Studies, and went on to write a trilogy of US-Mexico histories that became best sellers, one of which was the basis for a major film. I continued to write poetry; bit by bit the new synapses fired, and my writing seemed to flow. Or, as Dick Hugo put it, "It was almost like poems had piled up in me, and I just started writing and writing and writing...."

Today is Thanksgiving, a holiday not much celebrated in Mexico but one that we honor faithfully in our family in our Guadalajara home. So, it is appropriate that I finish this chapter with a note of gratitude for the grace which allowed the flickering candle of my art to keep burning. Terrance Des Pres once noted that:

> *Few of us believe anymore that through art our sins shall be forgiven; but perhaps it is not too much to think that through art a provisional state of grace can be gained, a kind of redemption renewed daily in the practice of one's craft.*

A final confession. A foolish but persistent resentment that I unfortunately retained was the note with a C grade ("Not honors work!") from Francine Prose back in 1977. Many years had passed, but the memory still cropped up from time to time there like an aching tooth. Such is the persistence of the ticks of a compulsive personality. I decided to do something about it. I began reading her work, including a novel entitled *Blue Angel* in which the protagonist is a creative writing professor. I enjoyed the novel and wrote an incisive review and sent her a copy when it appeared. She received it gratefully and we had a lovely exchange via email. One writer to another. One less resentment and a mind made freer and more creative in the process.

CHAPTER SIXTEEN

HIKING IN THE NORTH WOODS WITH JOSEPH BRUCHAC

Joseph Bruchac (1942—) is a poet, novelist, and publisher. He has written over 120 books and has been editor/publisher of the Greenfield Review Press in upper New York State for more than four decades. Well-known for his Native American storytelling drawn from his Abenaki identity, his novels for young people are popular in classrooms in the US and around the world.

The charismatic author and editor has been a part of my life for many decades now. A tall, muscular man, with a black belt in the martial arts, he is an imposing figure. His size and martial skills, however, are softened by a kind personality and a quiet, gentle voice.

I first came to know Joe through his work with the Committee of Small Magazine Publishers and Editors' (COSMEP) initiative to send books to prisoners throughout the US. Joe and his wife Carol were instrumental in the program. Bruchac had spent almost four years volunteering as a teacher in Ghana, western Africa, before returning to the Saratoga Springs area. Once back, he was hired to direct a Skidmore College outreach writing program for maximum-security prisoners.

In 1971, he and his wife, Carol, started the Greenfield Review Press, and since that time Bruchac has produced more than 100 books, many of them aimed at children. Along with his two sons, Jesse and James, and his sister Marge, Bruchac formed the musical group Dawnland Singers, which in 1995 opened for Bob Dylan and The Grateful Dead in Highgate, Vermont.

He invited me to his home in Greenfield Center, NY in the mid-Seventies to help edit an anthology of prisoners' works. His home was also the office of a highly successful publishing company.

We began to review submissions both from individual prisoners as well as work from literary magazines, prison publications, and PEN contest submissions, to choose the best pieces. We worked from 8 am until 1 pm, had lunch, then hiked in the woods.

Located just five miles north of Saratoga Springs, the Town of Greenfield is home to 8,200 residents in Greenfield Center, Porter Corners and Middle Grove, N.Y. It spans more than 41,000 acres of land bordering the Adirondacks.

Walking the quiet trails in the rolling foothills, we often went for half an hour or more without speaking. Occasionally, Joe would stop and admire a flower or plant and make a comment. We often came upon a rusted Coca Cola sign or a burnt foundation indicating that the primeval forest was gradually taking back bits and pieces of a community that had moved on.

In the evening, we shared our own poetry and stories and then back to work the next morning, reading, arranging and discussing selections. The completed anthology, *Light From Another Country* features the works of prisoners throughout the United States including poems and stories for which some of the authors had received the prestigious PEN Award, or a Pushcart Prize. The proceeds of sales allowed Joe's press to send free copies to prisoners, as well as other books on composition and collections of poems from well-known poets.

We both loved the poems of William Stafford and Robert Bly, and he enjoyed the works of several Native American writers such as Scott Momaday, Leslie Silko, Linda Hogan, James Welsh and Nila Northsun, all of whom I added to my growing reading list. Joe's name was on that list as well, of course. For his reading, I recommended the poems of Richard Shelton, Steve Orlen, James Wright, and Richard Hugo.

As we labored over the anthology, Joe and I formed a lasting friendship. We also decided that we would visit some of the prisons that we had sent books to. Subsequently we conducted intensive one-day workshops for prisoners in Michigan, Colorado, Pennsylvania, Arizona, and Washington. In addition, we both gave readings at storyteller conventions in Los Vegas, conducted summer humanities classes at Wayne State University, shared ideas and teaching methods, and solidified our friendship.

By the end of the Eighties, I had already published six chapbooks with various small presses around the country. Most of them had gone out of print after brisk sales. Joe and his wife Carol decided that they would remedy that. The Greenfield Review Press published my book *Making Our Own Rules: New and Selected Poems* in 1989. In a welcome review, Sam Hamill, writing from *Western American Literature,* noted:

> Michael Hogan is one of the best little-known poets in America. It's high time a reputable publisher brought out a large book of Hogan's work, one that will be kept in print for some time to come. His work is accessible, and we have much to learn from a poet of his intelligent modesty and character.

It was the first of many such reviews and landed me invitations to give readings throughout the United States and abroad. At some, I shared the platform with other fine writers; at others I was the solo presenter. It was the first time I also considered working outside the United States and within a year I would take advantage of an offer to teach and work in Mexico. Joe was instrumental in helping me make that decision.

At the time the book was published, he visited me in San Francisco, where I was asked to work with the inner-city schools as part of a program organized by the San Francisco Education Fund (SFEF), a group of businessmen who had organized to promote improvements in basic education. They wanted some fresh ideas. Over a dinner of hearty stew (Joe ate three bowls!) and two loaves of sourdough bread baked by my wife Lucinda, a talented artist and amateur chef, the three of us discussed strategies for my San Francisco challenge.

The local businessmen had complained that while the students in the top and middle percentiles who planned on college were doing fine, those at the bottom percentile did not even have the basic skills to work a cash register, place orders, or answer telephones properly. Many of the recent graduates were unemployable by the local businesses. Some were from broken families. Others had disciplinary records or were on probation for misdemeanors. Still others had addiction problems. They were classical "at-risk" kids. How could we combine these lower-performing students from all of the public schools into a group that would not be tagged as "remedial," a label they would resist and would further complicate student-teacher rapport and learning? How to find a way that would give them dignity as well as an impetus to do better? Joe proposed an idea similar to that of the prison writing workshops.

"It stands to reason that the skills we learned teaching prisoners should have some applications with at-risk students as well. Many of them come from the *barrio,* some even have fathers in prison. Your previous work in penal institutions would go a long way with establishing rapport."

Working with educator Quentin Baker at Washington High School, an enthusiastic teacher and organizer, we came up with a proposal. The students selected would form a group called the San Francisco Academy. They would have special classes taught by a business teacher, a computer teacher, and a writing teacher. They would write, edit, and format a literary magazine and get it printed with a grant from the SFEF. They would then sell the magazine through public readings which would pay off the cost of the grant. Although it would begin with students at Washington High, the program would be extended to other schools in the Bay Area as well, including the largely Latino population of the Mission District.

It was a resounding success. After one year and improved student outcomes, we published two fine literary magazines that were written, edited, produced and sold by students. As I was accepting congratulations from dignitaries who had attended the latest public readings by the participants, the mayor of San Francisco, Art Agnos, came up and shook my hand. "I hope this program goes on for many more years. Thanks for your leadership!"

"Thank Quentin Baker here from Washington High; it was really his idea," I replied. "I just came up with some ways of implementing it and taught some of the writing classes. But I hope you see what the major problem is, and how it has yet to be resolved. Perhaps no school can fix it on its own."

"What do you mean?" the mayor asked.

"Look around, Mr. Mayor. How many black or brown *adult* faces do you see? Notice most of the audience are officials, schoolteachers and administrators, and other students and teenage friends of the students who presented.

"Where are the parents?"

"Indeed. Where are the parents?"

Shortly after the graduation ceremony for our group, I met with the grandson of Alden Dow, the architect and founder of the Dow Creativity Fellowship visiting from the company headquarters in Midland, Michigan. He invited me to spend a month in Midland working on my next creative project and presenting to the Board there the results of my program. I agreed.

On the serene, wooded campus of the Northwood Institute, I wrote *A Writer's Manual for Inmates in Correctional Institutions* which was published by the Puffin Foundation and the Dow Creativity Center. It was a manual for prisoners to set up their own writing workshops, especially designed for those men and women who did not have access to visiting writers or outside programs. I went to several county jails, detention centers, and two prisons in Michigan and donated the books. I also met with wardens and other officials, as well as offering a few model classes to the prisoners. Later, the book was distributed free by the PEN Center in New York to inmates across the US.

Speaking with Joe Bruchac that summer, he reminded me of an earlier conversation. He questioned whether teaching at penal institutions and doing periodic readings and seminars at universities and schools was really my career path. "It seems to me that it is time-consuming, stressful, and takes its toll on your own writing and creativity. You've paid your dues in terms of volunteerism and being on the road. You need to start thinking about where you really want to spend your time and concentrate on your writing as well as another level of teaching."

Fortuitously, I had been contacted by Chuck Prince, director of the American School Foundation in Guadalajara, few months earlier, asking if Lucinda and I would be willing to come to Mexico to inaugurate a literary magazine there, as well as develop Advanced Placement classes at the US State Department-supported high school for that region. Following Joe's suggestion, we signed a two-year contract, and we were off to Mexico for a new adventure.

Sometime later when we had settled into our new home and I was experiencing both the joy of creativity and the satisfaction of having curious, disciplined students, I wrote to Joe and told him that I wished I had made the move to Mexico years ago.

"You probably weren't ready, years ago," Joe said. "Nothing worth anything happens quickly. Even an arrow shot from a bow which seems to take a split second actually took years of practice on the part of the archer. You get to where you need to be when you are ready. As an Onondaga elder once told me, *"You cannot pick strawberries until they are ripe."*

What was so uncanny about Joe's wisdom was that it also contained a reference which was meaningless to me at the time. It was not until many years had passed that I was invited by Des Sjoquist, the director of a school in British Columbia, that I met Onondaga students and parents, members of the Northern segment of the Iroquois Nation, the month the strawberries ripened.

CHAPTER SEVENTEEN

LATE NIGHT IN DETROIT WITH ETHERIDGE KNIGHT

Ethridge Knight (1931-1991) was an African American poet. His first book Poems from Prison was a literary success, and he became known as a major voice in the Black Power Movement. His subsequent nine books became popular due to his rich language and startling imagery, and also due to his charismatic readings at universities throughout the US where he attracted large crowds.

One of the most unexpected but pleasurable invitations to teach came one June morning from Wayne State University in Michigan. They asked if Joe Bruchac, Ethridge Knight and I would run the Summer Humanities session for GM and Ford employees. We all agreed and were given some guidelines but were essentially free to devise our own curriculum. I had heard about Knight and read a few of his poems and was interested in meeting him. Knowing his background, I was interested to see what he would come up with for his part of the curriculum. Joe, as I suspected, would be heavy into Native American contributions to American culture, contemporary poetry, and storytelling.

When Knight sent us his outline, I found it fascinating. As expected, there were a couple of African American authors, some speeches by King and Malcolm X, but there was also Emerson's "Self-Reliance," Thoreau's "Civil Disobedience," a short history of the Harlem Renaissance, and Cardinal Newman's "Idea of a University."

Resident musicians in Detroit were designing the music part of the curriculum, and local art historians were taking care of art and architecture through the ages. My role would be Latin American culture and history, as well as an introduction to British and American poetry.

It was one of the best groups of students I had ever taught. The auto workers were hungry for knowledge. Naturally they wanted the four credit hours that the course brought them; with their eventual degree they would gain promotion and wage increases. But beyond that there was also a genuine interest. Intellectual curiosity as well as enthusiasm was the atmosphere of these two-hour classes. In the evenings, we often met with groups of students and had pizza and beer or soft drinks. After that Joe usually headed home to make a call to his wife Carol, and early to bed, earlier to rise. I occasionally went over to Etheridge's apartment where I had cup after cup of coffee as Etheridge held forth on every subject from Chomsky's views on the media, the failures of the black Power Movement, surrealism of the French poets, and the magical realism of the Latin Americans. I remember we had a warm conversation about Borges, and Etheridge wanting to know why I didn't include him in my offerings on Latin American culture. I finally admitted my failure.

"Everyone is so damn excited about Gabriel García Márquez," he remarked. "Well yes. *A Hundred Years of Solitude*, I grant you, is something of a classic. But García Márquez wouldn't be possible without Borges. The ground was already plowed, and the seed sown. All he needed to do was tend a few plants and bring them to fruition. Borges created a path for Latin Americans similar to the one James Joyce created for the Irish with *Dubliners* and *Finnegan's Wake*. He paved the way for Seamus Heaney and the rest of that crew. Of course, no one in the US reads the foreigners anyway. I read somewhere that only ten percent of Americans buy a new book every year, and only 1 percent of that one percent buy a book by an author they haven't read before."

Finally, I was able to get a word in. "And most of the poets they do read are dead."

"Right! And get no royalties. Even worse. Most of their poems are in the public domain so not even their descendants get royalties. How fucked-up is that? The only people making money off books are the big-name publishers and most of them are owned by one or two conglomerate media groups."

"And they make their money off 'bestselling' romance novels."

"And bullshit books by presidents and politicians."

"Shit, man. This is a drag. Let's talk about something real. Like maybe Lucille Clifton's poetry or Rita Dove's, or maybe du Bois' short stories… I have an idea! Let's call my ex, Sonia [Sanchez] and see what she is reading these days."

It was now well after midnight. He dialed; it rang several times, but no one picked up.

"It's pretty late," I said.

"Wait, wait! I know someone who's up late. My other ex, Miss Mary.

"Hi, Babe, it's Etheridge. How are the kids?" (Etheridge and Mary McAlanny had adopted two children before their divorce. She currently had custody.)

"Good, good. I am here with Michael Hogan. You know, the poet from Arizona. Yeah. We were wondering who you are reading lately. Who? Ai? What kind of name is that? Yeah, so it's really Florence Anthony. You got her book there? Read us something, Babe. Please? I'll put you on speaker. Read us a couple of poems, and then you can hang up if you want. Promise."

Mary came on the speaker. "Hi Michael. You don't know of Ai either?

"Well," I said. "I know the name. She went to the University of Arizona, but I wasn't there during her years."

"Anyway," Mary went on, "Ai is part black, part Choctaw and part Japanese. Before starting college, one night during dinner with her mother and third stepfather, Ai learned that her biological father was Japanese. She was known as Florence Hayes throughout her childhood; it was not until graduate school, when Ai was going to switch her last name back to Anthony, that her mother finally told her more details about her past. Her mother had an affair with a Japanese man, Michael

Ogawa, after meeting him at a streetcar stop. Learning of the affair had led Ai's first stepfather, whose last name was 'Anthony,' to beat her mother until family intervened. So, when Florence discovered all this, she changed her name to 'Ai' which in Japanese means 'love.' So, her poems are *persona* poems; she takes on the personality of different characters. Some of them are men who are often violent, like her first stepfather. Others are ones who suffer abuse like her mother; many are violent and get revenge for abuse by killing the abuser."

Mary read us three poems: one about a prostitute who was beaten up by her john and ended up stabbing him; a history poem about the night the brownshirts smashed the windows Jewish stores in Berlin ("Kristallnacht"), and then another one whose ending I remember:

> *I'll give you a taste of black*
> *you won't forget*
> *For a while it will make you strong, make your heart lion,*
> *then I take it back."*

"Wow!" Etheridge exclaimed. "That bitch heavy. She got more nigger in her than jap, that's for sure. Where'd she learn to write like that?"

"I think her teacher was Richard Shelton," Mary offered.

"Damn! He was your teacher, too, wasn't he, Mike? Thanks, Miss Mary. You get some sleep now. Go kiss the lil' 'uns goodnight for me." He hung up the phone.

"So, Shelton's classes must have been somethin' else. Did you learn a lot? I mean, did it help your writing being in that MFA program?"

"I think more than anything, it *encouraged* my writing. It not only provided me with a safe place to write and feedback, but I was with people who felt that writing was important, that it was a vocation, not a pastime. Also, I met with people who were cultured and well-read and had a deeper sense of what it meant to be human and had contact with a wider world than I was exposed to. I wanted that."

"Yeah, poetry brought me that, too," Etheridge said. "I like to say I did it on my own, but I had my mentors and teachers too. Sonia, my first wife, was a poet and Mary, too. Dudley Randell visited me often in prison and we had one-on-one workshops. He brought me books. So did Madeline Brooks, another fine poet. So, I read all the black poets: Langston Hughes, Robert Hayden, James Mason, Rita Dove, Lucille Clifton, Dudley Randell. Then I read the Romantics like Keats and Shelly, and the Victorians like Browning, even some moderns like Auden. I think my favorite white boy was Dylan Thomas, though. And I also appreciated the power of Martin Luther King's prose. Though I thought he was a bit of a Tom, I wanted my voice to resonate like that, you know? So, yeah, I even read the Bible, especially the psalms and Matthew. I wanted that element of music in my poetry. I also want to have the power like Malcolm X or Huey Newton to move people with my words. So, I was attracted to the performance side of poetry. I love to read out loud to DECLAIM! Do you know my poem about what the Warden said?"

"Yeah, he said something like, 'Say, Ethridge, you're a trustee. How come you black boys don't run off when they have a chance like white boys do?' And you said, 'maybe because we ain't got nowheres to run to.'"

"Precisely, my man. More prisoners and ex-cons have begun to see themselves not as individual outcasts but rather as members of a social subclass. And, from this point of view, American society as a whole constitutes the primary prison for the underclass. "Don't be shocked," Malcolm wrote in his *Autobiography*, "When I say that I was in prison. You're in prison. That's what America means: prison."

And on and on into the night.

"Do you stay up this late every night, Etheridge?" I asked.

"You know, I was thinking. When I heard those poems of Ai. I'm glad I wasn't in that class. I don't want to explore that kind of darkness. I write about prison, sure, but I play it off. I use humor and irony. But I also witnessed some pretty horrible shit, like gang rapes, stabbings, and snitches being thrown off balconies, and one time a child molester being burned up in his cell, screaming. I don't want to think about stuff like that. And I would never write about it. That's tempting the devil, man. I remember several times when I first got out, I woke up screaming. Scared Sonia, and then Mary in her turn. Writing about that stuff is like playing with the Ouija board. Don't know what you might raise up."

"You don't really believe that do you?"

"Man, I don't know anything for sure. What do I believe? I believe there is evil that lurks in the hearts of men. I believe violence is random and often inexplicable. I witnessed cons who were bored and feeling helpless and wanting to make something happen. Sometimes they would say someone was a snitch even if he wasn't and sit back and watch him get killed. I seen an 18- year-old kid who was doing 24 months on a statutory rape change for making it with his 16-year-old girlfriend. Someone accused him of child molesting, and he was gang raped by four Aryan Brothers.

"Most nights I stay up till I pass out from exhaustion. Even harder now that I am off the needle. Just doing Methadone these days don't get you high. Just takes the edge off. But that's the only way I can sleep without dreams."

I think I finally went home at about 6 am, even then Etheridge had not quite wound down. Ethridge *breathed* literature and ideas and was a non-stop talker. His monologues were fascinating for the most part, full of prison stories, political ideas, references to literature, and scraps of poems. But as the darkness paled outside and the wind came up, I knew it was time to go.

Oddly enough, although he sipped whiskey steadily through the night and early morning, he never appeared physically intoxicated. Instead, he grew more and more loquacious and outrageous in his cascades of language as the dawn approached, and there was a great sadness in his eyes.

CHAPTER EIGHTEEN

IN THE TIME OF THE JACARANDAS

It was 1992 and my wife Lucinda and I had been teaching at a school in Guadalajara, Mexico, for two years, enjoying the climate, the people, and the students. Lucinda taught history, English, and logic at junior high at the American School, and I taught English and American literature and creative writing in the high school. I had recently been selected to be the department chair and had begun to make major changes in the curriculum. I loved my work and was excited to upgrade the academic offerings. Our house was only a few blocks from the school, and we welcomed the greetings of neighbors, *Buenos días, Maestros*! as we walked along the tree-lined streets each morning to work. It was a blessed time. The jacarandas were in bloom, shedding their lovely purple carpet across our street.

In my World Literature class, I added poems from Octavio Paz, Jame Sabines, Ruben Dario and others. Mostly in translation because it was a class taught in English, but I read the originals and also played recordings of their readings to attune my ear to Spanish.

One of my favorite poets was Jaime Sabines. I loved his work for its accessibility since I was still in my early stages of Spanish mastery. In addition to his works in our school library, I also had a copy of W.S. Merwin's fine translation, *Pieces of Shadow: Selected Poems*. So I could check my tentative understanding. I was fascinated by his humor which, combined with humility, produced such lighthearted poems as "The Pedestrian" in which he realizes that, although he had a notable reputation in foreign literary circles abroad, he was unknown in his neighborhood and unappreciated even within his own family. *They say you are a famous poet*, he said to himself feeling quite proud. But when he returns to Mexico, nobody on the street realizes he is a poet, much less at home. In Mexico with its heavy traffic the pedestrian is the least respected on the roadway. *That's it,* thinks Jaime. *I am a pedestrian.* Relieved of the need for importance, "he lies on the bed with the sweet happiness of contentment."

That was my feeling as well. A humble teacher who walked to school each morning with his wife, I had a sweet contentment. Then, on an otherwise uneventful Monday, I got a call from Colorado that my only son, Gary, had died suddenly. He was twenty-seven years old and in the prime of life. Like all such deaths it was meaningless, wasteful, absurd, and pointless. He was charming, intelligent; he was warm-hearted, eager and enthusiastic. Though he had a few setbacks in the past and some problems with substance abuse, he had been getting back on track and had shared with me his ambition to be an historian and perhaps teach at a university someday. He wanted to be a history teacher, and nothing I could say about poor salaries, low prestige, and long hours would dissuade him. But he died before his dream could be realized. After the grief, after the heartache, what shape could I give this death? I had no answers. His death left me bereft and rudderless. But each day when I arrived at school our principal, Miss Soledad Avalos, gave me a warm and heartfelt hug. She was a spiritual woman with a generous, caring heart and was known by students and faculty alike as "Miss Sol." Still, as the days went by, I realized that I had no inner resources to cope with my son's death. I was estranged from his mother who lived up north, and my new wife did not really know Gary, so her well-intentioned words of comfort rang hollow.

I came close to breaking down in class one morning and decided that I would submit my resignation from the school and return to the States. When I sat down with Miss Sol, I opened my heart to her. I expressed my gratitude for the trust with which she had endowed me, for the promotion to department head, and my regret that I could no longer work at the school as a teacher. I was simply too emotionally distraught and did not think I would be able to continue. She listened patiently and sympathetically. Then she got up and wrapped me in a warm hug that lasted more than a minute. I was not used to such intimacy from an administrator and was at first uncomfortable and pulled back. But she held on tight, and gradually I experienced a sense of peace and comfort.

I remembered then the lines from Sabines's poem which I had played from a recording of a reading he gave in Mexico City.

People who know how to give hugs

know that the object is not to encircle the other
with one's arms
but rather to touch your soul with theirs.

"Las personas que saben…"

When she resumed her seat, she told me, "I am so sorry for your loss, Michael. And I can only begin to imagine the depth of your grief. I have never lost a child. But I have lost someone whom I loved dearly, and I know that being around people who care for you, who love you, is important. Here at this school, you have come to be loved, and we consider you as part of our family. The students know that you are suffering and will bear with you. The faculty, too, have shared with me their hope that you will come out the other side of this painful experience and continue to work here. But I fully understand if you wish to leave.

"I would only add this. You are a very good teacher. One of the finest I have worked with. But you could be a truly great teacher if you could begin to see your son in the eyes of every child you teach. It would transform your classes into something special. You would leave a legacy which would be remembered for a long time. So please, for my sake, and the sake of those children, take a day or two to think about it. Talk it over with Lucinda and then go to a quiet place, maybe say a prayer, and then come back to tell me what you have decided."

We stayed. For more than three decades now. Whether it was Miss Sol's words, or the hug that Sabines's poem had prepared me for, or the love that I found among the Mexican people, it resulted in the meaning

I have chosen to add to my view of the world: to see the face of my son in every child I teach. I know we heal each other by our willingness to risk the hug, the openness, the sharing of our feelings, and—in the process—we come to see our son in everybody's son, our daughter in everyone's daughter.

*****

Por qué y para qué

Still, Gary's death was abrupt, meaningless, and left a gaping hole in my psyche that I knew would never heal, never scar over. For days I was numb, unable to work, to think, and went about my teaching duties in a haze. Teaching did keep me sane, though. I focused on the young people I was working with and learned to see my son in each of their faces. I suppose along the way I was becoming a more compassionate, more accessible teacher, and was certainly available to students after classes in a way I had not been before.

Spiritually, however, I was bereft. I hadn't completely lost every scrap of faith; remnants remained, but they were too fragile to be of any solace. Philosophically I was at the lower end of Sartre's definition of existentialism. Life was meaningless, absurd, and the death of a child was one more piece of evidence to prove that.

Then, amid this storm of spiritual negation, I experienced two epiphanies. The first was a poem by the Nicaraguan poet, Ruben Dario. The poem was a short one. A type of Jeffersonian acknowledgment of

Jesus by someone who saw him as a spiritual teacher rather than a part of the Trinity.

LITTLE POEM FOR JESUS

> *Everything you ever said*
> *Can be summed up in two words:*
> *Pay attention.*

 The second was an invitation to attend the funeral Mass of a colleague whom I did not know particularly well who had also lost a child. At the funeral, a Jesuit priest gave the sermon in Spanish. I was still in the process of learning the language, so I was often distracted when listening to long narrations in a second language. This priest, however, hit upon just the exact note that resounded like a Chinese gong in my consciousness. He said that when someone we love dies, especially someone young and who was in the prime of life, we often say; "Por qué? Why? Why did this happen?" Well, if we were truly honest, what we really are asking is "Why did this happen to me?" Because it is really about how their death affects us that we are speaking. The person who has died feels no pain, no regret, no remorse or hope for tomorrow. It is those of us who are left behind who are asking this question in the bleakness and hopelessness of our deep sorrow and loss. "Por qué? Por qué? Why has this happened to me? Why has this person been taken away from me? Why am I left with this hole in my heart, this emptiness in my stomach, this bleakness of everyday life?"

 "But the better question," the priest went on to say, "the question that we should be asking, the question that can change us and thus change the world, is Para qué? What can we make of this death? How can we create meaning out of this meaningless loss? For we, not God, are the authors of meaning—not fate, not the universe with its millions of galaxies streaming through space indifferent to our sorrows, our needs, and our terrible losses. So, para qué? What can I do to make sense of the senseless? What unfinished task did the departed leave behind that I can finish? What thought or inspiration did he or she have that I could emulate? What dream unrealized that I could fulfill? And when we find this, when we find a way to give that death a meaning, we will discover not only that the loss has become a more bearable part of our memory and everyday consciousness, but also that your loved one lives through you in a way that is both empowering and life affirming, and you have given to the departed soul a bit of immortality."

My son Gary loved studying history and all the elements that made up that discipline: chronologies, geographies, cultures, literatures, evolution of armaments, and political philosophies. His never to be realized goal in life was to become a historian.

After listening to the priest talk about para qué, I began to think about how my son's wish might relate to my own life. As a writer I was used to doing research, both to create fictional characters, and for the occasional nonfiction article. However, I had never done any extended work in history. When I received an appointment to teach at a school in Mexico, however, I discovered that one of my forebears had been a combatant in the Mexican Army resisting the US invasion of 1846. He was a member of a group called the Batallón de San Patricio, a military unit primarily composed of Irish immigrants who fought on the

Mexican side. I knew little about the group and there was only one published historical work on the Batallón in English and a short novella in Spanish. I read that material and searched for more. I realized that I would have to explore Mexican records of the 19th century, as well as visit the US and Irish archives. It was more work than I was willing to take on, since I was teaching full time and chairing two departments.

However, with my son's death and this new incentive from the priest's talk and the Dario poem's imperative, I began to firm up a commitment to begin that work in earnest. I realized that I needed a broader background in Latin American history before I could get anywhere, as well as a better knowledge of the Spanish language. So, I enrolled in courses at the Universidad de Guadalajara. That was the beginning.

During spring break and over the summer months I visited all the battle sites of the Mexican War. I interviewed descendants of the original Battalion. I conducted research in the Archivos de la Nación in Mexico City, as well as in the newspaper archives in the Hemeroteca Nacional de México (National Library) which housed the 19th-century daily and weekly journals. When our school introduced Week Without Walls, I had the opportunity to accompany a group of Mexican students to Washington DC, where I visited both the National Archives and the Military Archives there. Although I discovered a treasure trove of materials at the latter, I was unable to take the time to copy them since most were stored in boxes and not filed in any orderly fashion. Plus, since I was responsible for a group of students, I could not spend my time in Washington on personal matters.

When I explained my predicament to Michael Pilgrim, the archivist in charge, he sympathized and took down my personal information. Two months later he called me and said that he had put all the records on microfiche and would send them to me for a nominal fee. What a wonderful response and what a teaching moment for my students! As I told them at the time, when you do your work quietly and persistently, unknown friends will find you and angels will surround you.

The next year I had a similar moment when the archivist at the Museum of Interventions in Mexico City, (Museo Nacional de Intervenciones) allowed me free access not only to their archives, but their storage cellar in an old convent that was the locus of one of the last battles of the war. There I discovered a cache of American weapons (smuggled by Guatemalan gun runners after a burglary at Harper's Ferry) that had been hidden for over 150 years! Meanwhile, I continued my courses and three years later had a doctoral degree in Latin American history, a competency in Spanish, and a dissertation entitled "The Irish Soldiers of Mexico" that was rich not only in factual history, but in compelling narratives gleaned from my research.

I sent queries out to major publishers and finally one accepted my manuscript. After a year working with the editor, expanding, verifying sources, obtaining permissions for photos, reworking some of the academic language into a more popular narration, the manuscript was finally a book that we both agreed would be a major contribution to US, Mexican, and Irish history. But when the time came for publication, I was notified that the marketing division of the press projected that it was a "niche book" and, without a major buy-in from the Texas Board of Education, the largest purchaser of history texts, it would sell only a few thousand copies. They decided not to publish. I was devastated.

But I truly believed that this work was my son's legacy, and his death demanded that I find a way to make my book accessible to a wide audience. I was, thus, only momentarily discouraged, when my resilience of purpose set in. That evening, I went to a poetry reading at the University of Guadalajara and ran into an editor by the name of Emmanuel Carballo, who had a home in Ajijic and with whom I later had lunch at the Nueva Posada.

When he asked if I was working on anything new, I told him about the *Irish Soldiers of Mexico* manuscript and my trials with the publisher. He offered to read it and a few weeks later called me to let me know that he was excited about its possibilities as a book and thought it should be published. However, there was one problem. Lack of funding. He said I needed to get a co-sponsor in order for the Fondo Editorial Universitario to publish. He suggested that I give a presentation to the Heróico Colegio Militar, an organization similar to the West Point Alumni Association in the US but composed of Mexican general officers. If they were interested, perhaps they would underwrite the project.

Well, imagine! A gringo high school teacher giving a presentation in Spanish on Mexican history to a group of Mexican senior officers. How intimidating! But with my son's image in mind, I did so humbly yet enthusiastically. To my surprise, not only were the officers enthusiastic about the project, they provided a retired brigadier general,

Clever Chávez Marín, to translate the work into Spanish and also offered their facility for the formal book launch later in that year.

And so the unimportant niche book that was supposed to sell only a couple of thousand copies, sold out its first printing in less than 90 days and then went on to sell twelve editions in English and three in Spanish. It was a best seller on Amazon and held the #1 spot on Mexican (and Irish) history for several consecutive weeks. Even now, thirty years later, it continues to have brisk sales. It was also an inspiration for four documentaries, an MGM film starring Tom Berenger, and a commemorative postage stamp in Mexico and Ireland. I have since been invited to speak at all the major universities in both Ireland and Mexico on this little-known aspect of their mutual histories, and I am a consultant to the embassies of both nations.

Even more important, the book prompted a closer relationship between Mexico and Ireland, resulting in scholarships for Mexican students wishing to study in Ireland, increased trade between both nations (including the purchase of Mexican cement for use in Irish construction), Irish dance schools in Mexico, a mariachi group in Dublin, a popular music CD by the Chieftains, and a solidarity between both nations which continues to this day. Para qué? What meaning could I possibly create from my son's death? What might result from the attempt? The blessings far exceeded my fondest hopes. This inauspicious book dedicated to my son resulted in bringing two nations together and formed a solid bond of international friendship resulting in increased educational and business opportunities, cultural exchanges, and a feeling of goodwill. Para qué? That question has made all the difference and has never stopped resounding.

CHAPTER NINETEEN

HARVARD YARD WITH JOSEPH BRODSKY

Joseph Brodsky (1940-1996) was a Russian and American poet, essayist, playwright, and translator whose work was wide-ranging, exploring the human condition and the meaning of existence. His work was considered anti-Soviet by the repressive regime of the USSR at a 1964 trial, and he was sentenced to five years hard labor as a "social parasite." Upon his release he was constantly monitored by state censors and prosecutors and several times placed in mental institutions for "personality modification." In 1972 he was exiled to Austria and there, with the help of US Embassy officials, made his way to the States where he became a citizen in 1977. In 1987 he was awarded the Nobel Prize for Literature.

It was a chilly, overcast February morning in Tucson, Arizona, when I received a call from Steve Orlen. I had just returned from teaching a writer's workshop at the Washington State Prison state prison in Walla Walla, with the poet Bill Wilkins.

"Michael, you'll never guess who's meeting me in my office this morning!" Steve crowed.

"Let me see. Linda Ronstadt?" A real possibility since her father was a former sheriff and the family lived nearly. She was my fantasy in those days.

"Nope. Three guesses. Try again."

"Robert Bly?" A poet that we had requested the Poetry Center invite several times to no avail. The last time he read at the university was in the Sixties.

"No, no. It's a Russian!"

"Let me think. Umm. Brodsky? Yevtushenko? Solzhenitsyn?"

"Right the first time. Joseph Brodsky! He's giving a reading tonight. It will be bilingual. I'm doing the English version. Anyway, I told him about your work in the prisons and he said he'd love to meet with you. Are you free?"

I was. Within a half hour I was in Orlen's book-lined office where, behind a full ashtray and a cloud of cigarette smoke, sat a Russian in his late thirties, with a blocky build, balding, reddish-brown hair, and rimless eyeglasses. He spoke with a slight lisp. While he had no accent, sometimes his sentences were sprinkled with "well" which seemed a tic like "um" or "em", perhaps a holdover from a childhood stammer.

"It is good to finally meet you, Michael. Well, our friend Steve here sings your praises."

"No one needs to sing yours, Joseph. Your reputation precedes you."

"Too kind, too kind," he said, puffing on his cigarette.

We chatted about the weather at first. I had on a sweater and a windbreaker; Brodsky was in shirtsleeves. He said he preferred winters in Michigan to what he considered a mild (35-40 degrees) February in Tucson.

"But I would think you had enough of freezing in Siberia."

He laughed. "When I was sentenced to prison the judge said you will soon learn what it is to be a parasite in the Soviet state. You will suffer. Ha! What the judge didn't realize was that I had already lived and worked in Siberia in my youth as an assistant on a geological survey. I loved it! I found the cold weather invigorating. And well. Well, then he sentenced me to well...five years hard labor in Norendskaya in the Arkhangelsk District. Perfect! I knew people there; some were ex-prisoners but good people. Oh, and I had books, including English books...well, rrrr...Robert Frost, W.S. Auden, others, you know...well, the poems of John Donne even. Well, they were very difficult, but I was learning.

"I think probably I had it much better in Siberia than Americans in prison here! Well, you have brutal gangs which prey on weaker prisoners. You have blacks who are treated brutally by guards. You have white inmates who in turn are brutalized by black inmates who outnumber them five to one. All live in fear and anger, or resentment and mind-numbing boredom. There is little work and idleness provokes violence."

"And Siberia was different?"

"Very much so. We had barracks and some prisoners even had a small shack of their own. We worked on farms, repairing roads, clearing land, caring for livestock. I chopped wood in the morning, then milked the dairy cow, her warm teat against my cheek in the frosty morning, the moment of quiet solitude."

"Probably the most troublesome aspects of the US system are the overcrowding, and the indeterminate sentencing," I offered.

"Yes, in Russia we receive a clear sentence, 3 years, 5 years. And most are released sooner. In America it is 5 to 10, or 10 to life; then you depend on the parole board and luck."

"The worst part is not harsh conditions or even uncertainty," I said. "Despite what most people think. It is the loss of freedom, and separation from family, friends, and the real world."

"Yes, loss of freedom is the most painful. I often think that hell is not fire and brimstone, but simply a place which God has abandoned. And there were prisons like that in Russia, like the Kresty Prison in Leningrad, where I worked briefly as a morgue assistant. Horrible job! Stitching up bodies after autopsy. But, well, Siberia was not so bad for me. I was released after 18 months. Psychiatric hospitals were much worse. Horrible places. You never knew if you would ever get out."

The Reading

During our conversations Brodsky was mild-mannered, and his voice was soft and thoughtful. But the reading presented a different *persona* and a voice that was startling. The evening began with a lovely introduction by Lois Shelton, the director of the Poetry Center in which she also recognized Steve Orlen who was to be reading the English versions of Brodsky's poems. Initially she had thought Brodsky would read a poem first, followed by Orlen. At the last minute, Brodsky decided to change the order. He wanted a more dramatic effect, so he would read the Russian version after Orlen's English version.

It was Valentine's Day, and the first piece was a love poem dedicated to Brodsky's first love, Marina Basmanova, who was introduced to him by his mentor Anna Akhmatova. The English version was well-received in Steve's finely modulated voice. Then Brodsky read. Or rather sang and chanted in what was a soulful and heart-rending Russian original of a poem of unrequited love and loss. It was a very powerful and moving piece and what followed throughout the evening was more of the same.

It is impossible to do justice to the melodious effect of the poems in Russian, nor the evocative power of Brodsky's voice. I remember reading a *Time* magazine article which described how Yevtushenko held a crowd spellbound in Moscow's Red Square when he read "Babi Yar", the poem about the murder of 33,000 Jews in Kiev by the Nazis and their Ukrainian collaborators. Brodsky had the same gift. He could speak without a microphone and be heard throughout the building, and his voice reverberated in your brain after the poem ended.

Fast forward to Harvard

Almost two decades would pass before I would meet up with Joseph Brodsky again. Lucinda and I had been living in Mexico and teaching at the American School Foundation in Guadalajara for a couple of years where I was Chair of the English Department and founder of the literary magazine *Sin Fronteras*.

One evening I received a call from Greg Nagy, inviting me to come to Harvard to work with the NEH summer session: "The Greek and Latin Lyric." It carried a stipend and came with an apartment a few blocks from campus. Lucinda and I were delighted to go.

Greg Nagy (b. 1942—) is a professor and scholar. Author of sixteen books and dozens of scholarly articles, he is currently the Director of Hellenic Studies and Professor of Classical Literature at Harvard University.

Professor Nagy is the most popular professor ever to teach at Harvard, where he has worked since 1966. A recent on-line course of his garnered 27,000 registrants, so many that Harvard had to send out an urgent request for post-docs to work as assistants. So, it was a singular honor to be asked to come to Cambridge. At that time, he was Chair of both the Classics Department and the Comparative Literature Department. He and his wife, Olga Davidson, also a scholar, had worked for more than a decade as well as dorm parents at Harvard, so they could save up enough money to buy a small farm in New Hampshire just across from Robert Frost's home in Franconia.

It was during my second week on the Harvard campus that I ran into Joseph Brodsky smoking an unfiltered cigarette in front of the Widener Library. I wanted a smoke as well, so we stood together and chatted about our lives, watching the gardeners trimming the lawn, and the sprinklers on the far end catching the summer sunlight.

"So you are in Mexico, these days, I am told. And quite sober and healthy, I see. My friend Czeslaw Milosz said you did not look well the last time he saw you. Glad you are well, my friend. And Mexico, it has been good to you?"

"Yes," I replied. "Life in Mexico is very good. I teach literature and writing classes that I love. I am also studying Latin American history for my PhD and practicing Spanish. I have done some translations of Paz and Sabines."

"Well, you will also discover, if you have not already, that nothing is more congenial to a poet than to live in a culture not one's own. You develop perspective, humility, and a new respect for your own language as well as the one you are now learning."

We smoked another cigarette and then, I invited him to an open-air restaurant on Massachusetts Avenue (now called the 730 Tavern & Kitchen; I can't remember what it was called back then), and we engaged in people-watching after we ordered. He told me about a tragedy in his family, the death of his mother and how he found out from a long-distance phone call to his father. I told him of the unexpected death of my young son, Gary, when I was out of the country. We both brooded a bit.

"Well, that is the price of leaving the homeland. We leave behind those we love and sometimes grow estranged. And with that comes remorse. Things we wish we had said or done. But there is also something to be said for the choice to leave. Although I had to leave Russia, I was under no compulsion to come to America. I was first in

Austria, then France. I was invited to go to Israel. And to England. But none of those seemed amenable."

"For me, Mexico was the same. It promised a higher level of freedom, I felt. Also, the love of poetry was far more prevalent there, and the openness of the people."

"More than America?"

"Yes, ironically much more freedom than *the land of the free and the home of the brave*. And the openness to foreigners, more sincere."

"And America to me is much more that way than France or Israel."

"Plus, you had the language."

"And you are learning another language as well."

Just then a panhandler came by, asking for change. Within seconds, a Boston policeman, whose car was parked on a side street, came around the corner and intercepted him. "Hold up, Charlie!" he said. Let's not bother folks." He took out his wallet. "Here's a couple of bucks go get yourself a coffee and a croissant up the street."

"Well, that was a surprise," I said. "Community policing at its best."

"Would that the rest of the country were as enlightened! And yet it highlights the problems of a capitalist society. The income disparity, the runaway cost of property by corporate investors. Well…the lack of affordable housing. Not exactly a worker's paradise."

"Well," I countered, "Russia was a lot worse from what I've read."

"Very true, but although Stalin failed, it doesn't mean that Marx was wrong, you know. There is some middle ground still attainable. America almost found it during Roosevelt's time and then lost sight of the vision after Reagan. But the American intellectual who says so, is often marginalized in his country, no? Like Chomsky, for instance. So, freedom is relative."

"As the saying goes, Capitalism may be the worst economic system, except for all the others."

"Yes, that is quoted often to me. Also, *Shoemaker, stick to your last.* But the problem is that Americans confuse political systems with economic systems. A dictatorship like Stalin's is a political system. And socialist countries which are non-democratic are held up as failures of the economic system. Like Cuba or North Korea. But they are merely examples of a failure of totalitarian control. Not true socialism. Those same defenders of capitalism never look at democratic socialist countries like Finland or Denmark.

"I am no apologist for dictatorships of any kind. And that includes plutocracies, whether the groups of rich controllers are families of vast landholders in Nicaragua, or corporate families in America. None of them want a real democracy. If they did, there would be guaranteed bargaining rights, national health care, free education, public held utilities, profit sharing by employees. These are all things the people want. And isn't it, as Lincoln said, supposed to be a government of the people, by the people? How is it that 60% of your congressmen are millionaires? How is it that you only have two parties and neither of them are anti-war nor progressive? How is it that ex-prisoners (mostly minorities) can't vote? How is it that corporations are considered *people*? Ridiculous!"

"You've never written anything on this subject."

"Nor do I intend to. Self-censorship (which I learned too late in Russia, by the way), is a survival tool. Look at Noam Chomsky. Openly criticizing capitalists, war mongers, mass media and Zionists, he finds himself tagged as an antisemite, black-listed by all mainstream magazines in America."

"But he still gets his books published."

"But not by any major press like Harper & Row, Oxford, or Doubleday. His books are mostly published by small, independent presses like Haymarket, Open Media, or by French publishers like Lumiere. But let's talk about other things. You are working with Greg Nagy. I have read some of his work. Very impressive."

"Would you like to meet with him? Or maybe have dinner with Lucinda and me?"

"I wish I could, but I am only here to deliver a copy of my book *Watermark* to a colleague at the Center for Jewish Studies who has an interest in Venice. Well, that, and also to do a quick bit of research. The Judaica Division at the Widener Library has one of the world's greatest collections in the world."

"I always forget that you and Steve Orlen are both Jewish."

"Well, I am also a Christian poet. John Donne's poetry led me to that. I find his spirituality most compelling. Also, my two favorite poets (and friends) are Czeslaw Milosz and Seamus Heaney, both Catholic."

"How did John Donne lead you to that?"

Brodsky began to recite in a booming voice which startled the other diners who gazed at us in wonder.

> *"Batter my heart, three person God....*
> *Take me to You, imprison me, for I,*
> *Except you enthrall me, shall never be free,*
> *Nor ever chaste, except you ravish me.*

You know the poem?"

"Yes, of course," I replied. Then I recited two lines, but not quite so dramatically.

> *Reason your viceroy in me, should defend*
> *But is captive, and proves weak or untrue..."*

"Well, so you know. Reason does not help in these cases. It is merely a tool for self-justification and rationalization. I was too full of myself, and addicted to self-will, which kept me from having a truly spiritual life. Well, I think you know what I mean. Czeslaw told me you were once a very heavy drinker, to the point of foolishness. 'The Irish poet in the yellow tux,' he called you. A dangerous risk to your gift as a poet, as so many find out too late. Well...But now you are sober for many years.

The change came about, I suspect, through a spiritual experience of some kind. You were battered, no?"

"Yes, in AA we call it 'hitting bottom'. So, one accepts it is not willpower that got you sober. That didn't work. It was surrendering to a Higher Power. Keeps you humble."

"Yes, and humility is the gateway to spirituality. It takes a long time to learn that. Some people never do. Others must be battered by life to come to it. They are the lucky ones if they accept that the battering was the only way and are grateful. They are blessed. Such as you and I, Michael. Here is a scrap of a poem for you to eat your lunch with. It's from a piece of mine called "Song of Welcome.""

> *Here's your food, here's your drink.*
> *Also some thoughts, if you care to think.*
> *Welcome to everything.*
>
> *Here's your practically clean slate.*
> *Welcome to it, though it's kind of late.*
> *Welcome at any rate.* ("*Song of Welcome*")

We ate our lunch mostly in silence because he was hungry, and because I was thinking of a poem that I might recite for him. At a loss to recall one of my own that was appropriate, I quoted from Stafford's "A Ritual to Read to Each Other."

> *For it is important that awake people be awake,*
> *or a breaking line may discourage them back to sleep;*

the signals we give — yes or no, or maybe —
should be clear: the darkness around us is deep.

We finished our lunch and smoked a cigarette. Then he had to go. We said our goodbyes, exchanged a warm embrace, and then retreated to our separate worlds.

****

Later I would write this poem:

> *You knew yourself an outsider at birth*
> *as we stood together in Harvard Yard:*
> *the maples with the seeds helicoptering down,*
> *sprinklers rainbowing the gravel walks,*
> *while we shared poems and smoked one cigarette after another*
> *unfit and bizarre in the healthy air*
> *like immigrant gardeners after trimming a Cambridge lawn,*
> *while students passed us in self-righteous haste*
> *as if they had someplace to go.*
>
> *But we were already at home*
> *each in our separate worlds*
> *creating a landscape congenial.*
> *And the cultures we left behind*
> *faded like a distant beach*
> *in the wake of a sailing ship catching a fair wind*
> *running clean, with full sail.*   *("Joseph Brodsky, 1993")*

CHAPTER TWENTY

DREAMING OF HORSES WITH JANE HIRSHFIELD

Jane Hirshfield (1953-) A poet, translator, and editor, was born in New York City, educated at Princeton University, and received her lay ordination from the Zen Center in San Francisco. The author of twelve collections of poetry, she has garnered numerous awards and honors. Her poetry utilizes commonplace language crafted into images that unite the natural world with the psychological and spiritual, the mystery of what is only partially known. She has read her work in venues in Europe and Asia and has been feted by audiences worldwide. In 2004 she received the Academy of American Poets fellowship for "distinguished achievement," the highest honor conferred by her peers.

For me one of the great things about living in the southwest was the wide-open spaces, and the joy of working with horses. My friend Susan North owned a small ranch in Tucson that I visited several times a week and in turn helped with chores. When Lucinda and I moved to Mexico, we lived in a small guest house on Rancho Contento next to a communal *ejido* where I rode horses.

Much like our own species, horses have different personalities, but they often reflect those of their human companions. At least I found it to be so. The horses I became friends with and rode across fields and deserts were tolerant, intelligent, sometimes willful and moody, but more often exuberant with a lust for life. Grooming them (curry comb, hard brush/soft brush), saddling them, riding them, sometimes just hanging out together in the stables; I often found myself seeing the world through their eyes. What a joy then to connect with the poems of Jane Hirshfield, who writes vividly about our equine companions.

In her poem "Heat" the narrator describes the behavior of her mare when she is in estrus, ready to be bred, and how she waits by the corral gate in the hopes that it will soon be opened, and she will get to run free and find the stud she hopes will be waiting. But it will not happen this time.

Not a stallion for miles, I'd assure her,

give it up.

But then the narrator turns inward and says to herself, "Oh, I knew how it was for her and easily

> recognized myself in that wide lust:
> came to stand in the pasture
> > just to see it played.
> ...the fence, the fence
> only a gap to open
> the width of a mare,
> the rest would take care of itself.
> Surely, surely I knew that,

> *who had the power of bucket*
> *and bridle—*
> *she would beseech me, sidle up,*
> *be gone, as life is short.*
> *But desire, desire is long."*

The frankness, the humor, the quick turn in this piece make it a delight to read. We see, without any overt telling, the connection between the outer reality and the inner self. How nature encompasses us, although we sometimes think we are its masters, and delude ourselves that we are aloof from its restrictions.

I have sometimes encountered horses tangled up in barbed wire, and I understand the historic conflict caused by imposition of agriculture on the once-open range of the West. It gave me a clear understanding of the vicious rivalry between newly arrived farmers and the established ranchers in the 19th century. I have written about the trauma of caring for an animal injured this way, and understand intimately the rancher's anger. In my poem "Learning" I bear witness to the horse's suffering, as I recoil from anger and move to caring and reluctant acceptance.

> *On the east side below the ridge,*
> *rich grass awash in shade,*
> *a roan colt has strayed and now lies twisted*
> *in three strands of rusted barbed wire.*
> *Her whinny a mere bleat as the mare*

nuzzles her torn flesh.
Her gangly deer legs useless and ripped
as flies feed feverishly on the blood.
She has been here for hours
and her eyes, white with panic
rheum over in the midday sun.

I know, taking the wire cutters from my belt,
watching the mare's eyes darken with trust,
that yellow salve will heal the cuts.
That water and rest by the shade of the eucalyptus
will bring her back to the world
sensible and clear
where hoofbeats drum a call to the hills
and the stallion snorts his musky warning.
She will gallop once more over plowed fields.

The mare nuzzles my hand as
I clip the bottom strands
and the colt trembling rises.
New hair will grow over the worst of it.
But looking at the mare's own scarred muzzle and torn ear
I know what will remain:
to grow content with dry tufts in the field that is hers;
to know those careful limits
freedom's early scars impose.

It is a decent poem, I think, and feels true even after many years. But I discovered later that Hirshfield had written a different (and perhaps better) poem with a similar theme. Although we were not in direct contact, her poem proved to be a twin to mine which, while acknowledging scars, suggested a transfiguration of sorts, and that somehow, the natural world partakes of the spiritual. Here is a fragment of her response:

> And see how the flesh grows back
> across a wound, with a great vehemence,
> more strong
> than the simple, untested surface before.
> There's a name for it on horses,
> when it comes back darker and raised: proud flesh.

Hirshfield does not stop there with the horse. She reaches the end of the poem with a leap that carries the reader into human relationships which have their own wounds and resultant scars, and yet can be what binds us in forgiveness and healing.

> And when two people have loved each other
> see how it is like a
> scar between their bodies,
> stronger, darker, and proud;
> how the black cord makes of them a single fabric
> that nothing can tear or mend.   ("For what binds us")

It was not until 1995 that I had the pleasure of finally meeting Hirshfield. I was working in Mexico when I received an invitation to speak at a College Board conference in Tucson, Arizona. Even though the honorarium was minuscule, I was happy to accept because it would give me the opportunity to visit Steve Orlen and Richard Shelton, and, I hoped, would allow me to connect with Barbara Kingsolver, who lived there with her husband part of the year. She had written a profile of me for *Tucson Weekly* magazine, and I wanted to thank her in person.

It turned out not to be. When I checked at the Poetry Center, they told me that Kingsolver was out of town. "But...Jane Hirshfield is giving a reading tomorrow night and then a master class the next day!" the secretary exclaimed. Well, I knew, as the secretary did, that we were in for a treat. Unfortunately, the master class, which I would have loved to audit, was at the same time as my college Board talk. Still, I managed to attend the reading.

The university had changed since my student days. More high-rise buildings, more cars, more students. It was winter and even in Tucson it can get chilly. There was an arctic nip in the evening air as I and a dozen teachers from our conference made our way to the auditorium. I was not surprised in speaking with them that several had used one or more of her poems in their literature classes. We talked about our favorites and those that seemed to work well with teenagers.

There was a capacity crowd, and we teachers formed a solid clack down front. I supposed we were a bit more vocal because we felt ownership of some poems as we had shared them for years with students.

Hirshfield did not disappoint. Not only did she read some more horse poems, which we teachers at schools in the Southwest and in Mexico particularly enjoyed, but she read one which worked particularly well with students. It was called "The Gift." In it the narrator feeds a ripe pear to her horse. The stallion takes it "first with whiskered lips and then teeth" but

> *soon it is no longer*
> *fruit but goes into*
> *betweenness and vanishment,*
> *turning to pastern*
> *and tail and good wall of the hoof*
> *and small tithing of gold*
> *for the pasture*

The teachers exchanged *sotto voce* comments based on their shared proprietorship. "Small tithing of gold" for horseshit! My kids love that one," commented one. We all nodded in agreement.

> *and he is careful even in greed,*
> *even in undignity*
> *of his foolish—no, it must be*
> *named true—his entirely goofy adoration*
> *and long-tongued worship of pears;*
> *when he knows what is pear,*

what is hand, when he looks
in my face as he chews and the crush
slobbers out and foams bright as spent happiness
onto my foot, onto my sleeve…

"Who knew you could use' slobber' and 'goofy' in a serious poem? She somehow makes it work."

"Her words shock you into paying closer attention," whispered my companion. I agreed enthusiastically. I loved this poem as well. We started the applause meter at the end of this poem, although most of the audience didn't "get it" as thoroughly as we did, or at least so we felt, because their response was merely polite.

After the reading, we had a chance to speak with her after the book signing and refreshments. She was frank and open, and genuinely interested in our take on "student-friendly" poems. She was grateful for this sharing and the time and space she generously provided. She told us, "What you tell me is so reassuring. I feel like we are all in the same story, and when we connect with a poem, it is because we recognize a piece of our own story being told and we see it clearly."

"I also think," said another, "that after the students have explored the poem on their own, when the teacher expresses her feelings, the students feel free to do that as well and they find touchstones that they didn't see or feel on the first or second reading."

"I agree," I replied. "That works sometimes. But it is a kind of didacticism I usually only explore reluctantly and early in the year. As the students gain confidence in their own explorations, I usually just let them go ahead and talk it out, even with a poem that they felt did not speak to them at all on first or even second reading. I am thinking now of one poem which worked very well with my students on the third reading."

"Which one is that?" she asked, smiling. "I always love hearing which of my poems connects with young people."

"Well, it is one of your short poems which truly delighted me. The narrator is walking alone on a wooded path going over everything that happened during her day. She has a "cold heart," something has upset her, spoiled her day. Then …

> *Willfully…*
> *I took a stick,*
> *lifted it to the opposite side*
> *of the path.*
>
> *There, I said to myself,*
> *that's done now.*
> *Brushing one hand against the other,*
> *to clean them*
> *of the tiny fragments of bark.*

"I assigned it as a homework assignment along with some others by contemporary poets. When we came to discuss that one, well, let's say at first there was little discussion at first. Comments varied.

"Yeah, I read it but it's like 'so what?' She took a stupid stick. Dumb."

"This is one of those poems that makes no sense. It doesn't go anywhere. What's the theme supposed to be? I don't get it."

Some smiled. Others were not so sure. I resisted putting in my authoritative take on the poem. They were on their own. After a pregnant silence, one girl volunteered:

"Maybe something happens because of the stick? Maybe, you know, like when you are stuck on something, like resenting somebody, if you do something different instead of dwelling on it, it can change how you feel?"

"Like start your day over, you mean?" another chimed in.

"Yeah," said one of the boys. "I like the word 'willfully' that she uses. You know, if you have a shitty attitude that is willful. So why not be willful in the other direction. Like to think positive."

"Not easy to do when you're pissed off, bro. Think positive, huh!"

"Well, this sounds silly, but you know sometimes when I get really pissed at my parents, I volunteer to wash the dishes after supper to work off my frustrations. I like the look on their faces when I clear the plates. It is a kind of revenge. Look I'm being mature and responsible, and you are being idiots. And when I finished stacking the clean dishes and wiping off the table, I feel like something has changed. I'm no longer angry and sometimes I even forget what brought on that feeling in the first place."

Another girl responded, "I know what you mean. Since you can't get yourself to change a mood, you can choose to do something else besides dwell on your negative feelings."

"And that can change your mood for you!"

"And it can be anything. Washing dishes..."

"Moving a stick from one side of the path to another...."

One of the Arizona teachers asked, "Was this one of your Advanced Placement classes? It sounds like a sophisticated and spirited discussion."

"Actually, no," I said. "It was a ninth-grade class at the American School in Guadalajara. For most of the students (sixteen out of twenty), English was their second language. But all of the students were told that when doing their homework, they were to read the poem once silently, then once out loud, then look for any place in the poem where they discovered something they did not know, felt something that moved them, or something that puzzled them. I knew that if enough of them did that, they would find their own way into class discussion or essay writing. I reminded them that sometimes it takes more than two readings, so to take their time, and not rush on to the algebra homework after two quick reads. And always read aloud."

"So that they hear the meter of the poem, the variation of the syllables, the clash of the consonants? The music?" Hirshfield asked.

"Yes, all of that and more. The *tone* which is not quite as easy to discern for young readers."

"And yet you let them explore on their own?" Hirshfield asked, clearly fascinated by this pedagogical conversation.

"Pretty much. I occasionally intervened, but I tried to hold my tongue as long as possible. What I have learned through experience is that when I step back the students will often find their own way. It seems haphazard, but it is actually organic, although the occasional Socratic question is often useful."

"Do you know," Hirshfield smiled. "I have been inexplicably happy since my plane landed in Tucson. I can't fathom why this is so. But I do know that talking with you and your fellow teachers has deepened that feeling."

It was a remark that went beyond basic politeness. It was heartfelt and embracing and left us all with a warm feeling for this poet who shared her passion for poetry, and her respect for those of us teaching young people ways to love it as well

CHAPTER TWENTY-ONE

A CLEAN WELL–LIGHTED PLACE WITH SAM HAMILL

Sam Hamill (1943-2018) was an American poet, founder of Poets Against the War, and co-founder of Copper Canyon Press. He was the author of a dozen books of poetry as well as a translator of poetry from the Chinese. A moral force in the US for peace and social justice, no stranger to political controversy, he famously refused an invitation from the White House during the Iraq War. He was awarded the lifetime Achievement Award by the Washington State Poets Association.

I think Hayden Carruth put it best when he said, "No one—I mean no one—has done the momentous work of presenting poetry better than Sam Hamill."[5] As an editor, publisher, public face of poetry in America, as well as translator, reviewer and critic, he has helped many other poets to be seen and heard including some of the most marginalized. What is even more amazing is that he has done all this and also produced fourteen volumes of poems, and two dozen books of translations.

---

[5] https://poets.org/poet/sam-hamill

The first book of Hamill's that I reviewed was *The Calling Across Forever* (1976) which whetted my appetite for more. The influence of Zen Buddhism was apparent in his work and made me curious as I went on to read more of his poems as the years passed. I discovered that he had in fact translated poems from Chinese and Japanese masters, including Li Po, Lao Tzu, Bashō, and many others. We corresponded off and on for the next three decades and shared our enthusiasms, contacts, and friendships. He was co-founder with Tree Swenson of Copper Canyon Press, formed originally in Denver but moved to Port Townsend, Washington, shortly thereafter. Over the course of thirty years, he would publish poets that I knew and befriended, such as W.S. Merwin, Lucille Clifton, and Norman Dubie, but also writers I had never encountered before such as Octavio Paz, Eleanor Wilner and Pablo Neruda, broadening my narrow but ever-widening world. Even more important for me as a human being, he opened possibilities of spiritual growth which had not been accessible to me before and for which I will be forever grateful.

During the Vietnam years we exchanged both letters and phone calls; one of the latter was a long conference call with Bill Merwin, in which we discussed our possible responses as writers to the Vietnam war. What would be our strategy? While we were appalled at the brutality and callousness of the American prosecution of the war: the lies that led to the Gulf of Tonkin Resolution, the bombing of Hanoi and the wanton destruction of infrastructure and civilian lives, Bill was reluctant to be classified as a political poet. "There was no doubt," he said, "that we should participate in public protests, write letters to our leaders in Congress, and for the newspaper Op Eds."

But should poetry be used as a political tool as well? Bill had his doubts. He felt that most political poetry was bad poetry to start with mainly because you have the sense that you're right and you're trying to tell your readers what's right. He argued that this was a kind of fundamentalism based on emotion. "It merely separates the world into two camps."

Sam, on the other hand, argued that there was a place in poetry for war protests. And that the emotion expressed in them was valid as well. But how to combine the two, and not merely be ranting and raving like the Free Speech Movement at Berkeley with Mario Savio and his gang which alienated the center and the right and—in addition—was not poetry but rhetoric?

I shared that point of view and was also troubled by the question. "Yes, that's preaching to the choir as they say, and just widens the divide. But I think that expressing that emotional energy you mention is valid and, as William James observed, translating that emotion into action is valuable in any sphere."

"But how do we avoid spewing out the unchecked emotional rant?" Merwin asked. Then proceeded to answer his own question. "Perhaps Wordsworth suggests an answer. Do you remember Wordsworth's definition of the origin of a poem? It is 'emotion recollected in tranquility.' Maybe that's our answer. Live with the emotion for a bit and then reflect. Think about the history of the war.

Think about a specific incident or a specific victim, or an image which disturbs you. Think about the ironies. If we do this, we might find that we have already written a piece which might be called political in the sense that any exploration of the subject is such, but it would also be good poetry."

I would remember that phone call many years later, long after the war in Vietnam had ended.

Fast forward to 2003. As Dwight Eisenhower had predicted, the military-industrial establishment had grown even more powerful over the years and the Bush Administration based on false "intelligence" and encouraged by a bellicose Chief of Staff, and a complicit Congress funded by the armament industry, planned an invasion of Iraq to begin that spring. The goal was to "eliminate the store of weapons of mass destruction" (which never existed). Shades of Gulf of Tonkin in which the defense department hastily manufactured an incident and a *casus belli* claiming that an American ship had been attacked by North Vietnamese patrol boats when it was not.

In January of that year Laura Bush asked Sam Hamill if he would help her organize a symposium of poets to celebrate "Poetry and the American Voice." It was to be a colloquium of poets and writers gathered to commemorate the long tradition of American poetry including the works of Walt Whitman, Emily Dickinson, Langston Hughes, and others. She felt that she was offering Sam a great honor and privilege to be thus selected to head up the event. Sam demurred. He felt insulted, not flattered. He was a Marine who knew the brutality of war and had joined Veterans Against the War during the Vietnam years. Now here was her husband, George, along with his pal, Secretary of Defense Rumsfeld, and others launching another unjust war on a pretext which would result in many thousands more dead, wounded or maimed for life, and scar a land and a people far from our comfortable shores.

Instead, Sam sent out emails to many of us requesting that we protest by organizing readings or by submitting poems to an anthology for a group he was organizing called Poets Against the War. Later he would send a link for the site where one could submit poems. Within a very short time he and his co-editor had collected over 15,000 poems, written by well-known poets such as Rita Dove, W.S. Merwin, Adrienne Rich, and Billy Collins, as well as poems from veterans, teachers, doctors and students.

When the White House heard about the site, the symposium was canceled. Sam and several others went to Washington anyway and held their own reading there. I was in Mexico and could not go but gave a speech at the American School Foundation on Peace Day which was attended by over 3,000 faculty, parents, teachers and the American consul general. In my talk, I questioned the justification for the war, suggested that a more temperate policy was called for, and quoted the words of Martin Luther King that "hate cannot drive out hate, only love can do that." Within the hour the US Consulate asked the director of the school for my resignation. She refused.

I heard later that in addition to his powerful poem on the self-immolation of a Buddhist monk in Vietnam, Sam also read my poem which was a tribute to a fellow Marine.

ANOTHER REASON FOR LOVING MOTHERS

For Sgt. Tom Valle, USMC

The two-note call of mothers
for sunburnt children at the beach--
prolonged, high-pitched at the end--
is a bittersweet sound, old as time.
A friend wounded by a mortar shell
said the last thing he heard
before the red blazing in his brain
was his mother's desperate call: BOB-EEEE
and then nothing.

How he struggled
through all those weeks of darkness
running against the tangled bushes of his dying
to be home in time for supper.

And a bit from Sam's moving poem on the self-immolation by a Buddhist monk:

What can it possibly mean
to make such a sacrifice, to give one's life
with such horror, but with dignity and conviction?

And my friend said simply, "Thich Quang Duc
has achieved true peace."

And I knew that night true peace
for me would never come...
The suffering world
Is mine, mine to suffer in its grief.

Bill Merwin took a more restrained and ironic look with his short poem, "After the War is Over" where he wrote:

When the war is over
We will be proud of course the air will be
Good for breathing at last....
The dead will think the living are worth it we will know
Who we are
And we will all enlist again.

We'll leave the final irony to former president George W. Bush himself in 2021 when he condemned Russia's attack on the Ukraine:

Speaking of preemptive strike on Kiev, Bush mistakenly referred to the decision to launch an "unjustified and brutal invasion of Iraq" before quickly correcting himself to say "Ukraine," in what was a bungled criticism of Russian President Vladimir Putin. As he put it:

"The result is an absence of checks and balances in Russia, and the decision of one man to launch a wholly unjustified and brutal invasion of Iraq," said Bush, before catching himself and shaking his head. "I mean -- of Ukraine."

Realizing his mistake, Bush then appeared to say under his breath, "Iraq, too."

As the French say: *plus ça change, plus c'est la même chose.* Which could mean, "the more things change, the more they remain the same," or "the answer my friend, is blowing in the wind." Take your choice.

Sam had a tough time in his final decade. Like many Americans who worked in the gig economy, he was under-insured and suffering from an illness that was terminal but slow. Chronic Obstructive Pulmonary Disorder (COPD) took its toll in his later years with its costly medication, inhalers, and oxygen therapies, and treatments. Many of us responded to an appeal to help him meet the expenses and he was blessed with a couple of lucrative readings in Italy and at San Miguel de Allende in Mexico.

We were quite close in that last decade, and I had spoken to him often both in the planning and later during his visit to Mexico. He expressed regret that he had not been able to publish my collected poems, or even the first five books, a project similar to the collection of Merwin's early chapbooks. It was on the drawing board at Copper Canyon, but Tree Swenson nixed it and then Sam left the press after several disagreements with the Board.

When the collection finally saw light thanks to Jim and Tanya Hepworth of Confluence Press, in 2012, Sam provided the introduction. The words he wrote for me, I would like to pass on to him and his memory. "These are poems that bear the weight of hard experience together with the sweet light of an open and generous heart." Oh, Sam. The open and generous heart was yours, and we all drew a deep and painful breath when yours stopped beating.

CHAPTER TWENTY-TWO

SANTA BARBARA WITH RAY BRADBURY

Ray Bradbury (1920-2012) was an American author who wrote in a variety of genres: poetry, popular fiction, screenplays, and essays. He also wrote science fiction, fantasy, and horror stories. His best-known works are The Martian Chronicles and Fahrenheit 451. Although in recent times he has been hailed as the Norman Rockwell of American literature in a dismissive fashion by some critics, his impact on young readers continues to be significant today, and the beauty and lyricism of his best work has stood the test of time.

I read my first Bradbury short story when I was nine or ten years old, probably in *Weird Tales* or one of the other popular pulp magazines of the day. As a teenager I devoured his popular novels and enjoyed them. One book in particular brings forth a recurring memory even today. *Something Wicked This Way Comes* (whose title is drawn from the witches in Macbeth) haunts me still when I see an elderly woman pass on the street. In the novel the young protagonist sees Miss Foley, his aging 7th grade teacher, who was determined to appear young, succumb to an evil magician who ran a carousel which, when ridden in reverse, could take years off your life and make you young again. After far too many circuits around on the device, she dismounted, and was now a helpless child of four, frightened out of her wits. With no one to help her, she curled up into a ball of despair and horror.

But the book which made a lasting *positive* impact on my life was *Dandelion Wine*. Published in 1957, I received the hardcover version hot off the press as a birthday gift from my parents along with a new pair of tennis shoes (called sneakers in those days). I was 14 years old and planned on trying out for the junior varsity football team at De La Salle Academy when I entered ninth grade. In the meantime, I was working a summer job with a landscaping company wearing work boots during the day, planting trees, digging irrigation canals, and cutting grass. But after 4 PM when I got home, I would take off the heavy boots, put on my "sneaks" and go shoot baskets, or I would run to the local grocery to get a loaf of bread and a pound of ground beef for my mother, jumping hedges and low fences along the way, running a broken-field route from the store to my home carrying the paper bag of bread and meat like a football under my arm.

In Chapter 5 of the book, Douglas, the 12-year-old protagonist, sees a pair of new sneakers in the shoe store downtown. He persuades the owner of the store, Mr. Sanderson, to try them on himself. "How can you sell something you haven't tested?" Persuaded by Douglas' description of how young and energized he will feel, Sanderson agrees.

Now, he says, feel those shoes…. feel how fast they'd take me. Soon as I get those shoes on, you know what happens? Bang! I deliver your packages, burn your trash, run to the post office, telegraph, library.

You'll see twelve of me going in and out, every minute…feel how fast they take me.

Impressed by the rush of words and images, and by his own youthful memories as he wriggles his toes and bounces a bit, Mr. Sanderson lets the boy have the sneakers in exchange for doing chores and making deliveries. "Antelopes, gazelles," Sanderson thinks after the boy has left. These are the images that remain in his mind, and mine as well these many years later. The lovely evocative language has all the earmarks of poetry.

Was Ray Bradbury a good poet?

Many people thought so, including Bradbury himself. The critic Christopher Isherwood praised his work as being more mainstream than other pulp writers back in the early 50's. *Time* magazine called him the "Poet of the pulps." And most importantly, Aldous Huxley, whom Bradbury met for lunch one day told him, "You know what you are? You are a poet." Bradbury took this to heart. After all he loved poetry, had a great English teacher in high school who inculcated in him a fascination with the genre, and was a member of the local Poetry Club as a teen with all the razzing that would have called forth back in the American high school of his day. Yet…all of the praise was not for his *verse*, which most had not read and that was derivative and mediocre with only the occasional redeeming feature. It was for his *prose* which was rich in imagery, original metaphors, and highly evocative flights. So, yes, he was a fine "poet in prose," especially in the short story and what we now call "flash fiction." His best novels, including *The Martian*

Chronicles, Something Wicked This Way Comes, and *Dandelion Wine* are all linked flash fiction episodes that form a novel. His novels are not the extended, carefully plotted genre as we had come to know it. As a matter of fact, Bradbury disparaged those who would attempt to give plotting advice to budding fiction writers. "Just take an interesting image and see where it leads you," he would offer. And that, in fact, is the strategy employed by many of the best authors of poetry.

Writer's Conference

When I was invited to present at the Santa Barbara Writers' conference, I was delighted to discover that in addition to T.C. Boyle, Fanny Flagg, Clive Cussler, and other notable invitees, Ray Bradbury was to be there as well. This major conference, now in existence for 40 years, was more than the West Coast equivalent of Bread Loaf. It included a much wider variety of writers, agents, and artists from Elmore Leonard, Charles Schultz ("Peanuts"), to Jonathan Winters and Gore Vidal; from William Styron and T.C Boyle to Robert B. Parker and Dean Koontz. Movie stars such as Eva Marie Saint and Bo Derek occasionally showed up. Highbrow and middlebrow alike: writers, actors, cartoonists, and movie executives often mixed. I ran into Lance and Conrad Hool there, the brothers who produced and directed *Man on Fire* (2004) with Denzel Washington. I had worked with them in 1998 on a movie called *One Man's Hero* with Tom Berenger, a film about the Irish in the Mexican American War where I was hired as a historical consultant and my book, *The Irish Soldiers of Mexico,* was a background source for the revised screenplay.

I looked forward to meeting Bradbury. He was one of my favorites as a teen and I thought of him fondly. I also knew, however, that we differed widely on politics. He was a Republican conservative; I was a progressive Democrat. He thought the MFA programs were useless and that writers learned on their own or not at all. He dismissed the value of a university education for authors since he did not go to college himself and did quite well without it. What we had in common though, I hoped might transcend those issues. We were both life affirmers and lovers of language. We both felt a vocation to share our love of both the bright and dark sides of life with unrepressed energy and discipline. We were both early risers who believed in coming to our desks and writing a bit each day. We both had mentors whom we honored.

Unlike other conferences which were held at convention centers or writing retreats, this one was held at a Christian university, Westmont College. There was no wet bar on campus to the disappointment of many but quite acceptable to me since I had given up drinking several years earlier and did not enjoy being around conference attendees who imbibed too freely and were often loud and obnoxious. The food was excellent, plentiful, and well prepared, and the surroundings were conducive to long nature walks and meditation, or quiet conversations.

The Campus

Lying just to the east of the city of Santa Barbara, which has the largest south-facing coastline on the Pacific, Westmont College is in an ideal location. Nestled beneath the steeply rising Santa Inez mountains, its climate is Mediterranean, and the area is often described as the

Western Riviera. The campus has no real rival in beauty with its stunning architecture, picturesque location, and wooded surroundings. Only Salve Regina University situated on the rugged cliffs of Newport, Rhode Island can come close. But even those converted Gilded Age mansions and the Cliff Walk along the wild Atlantic come in second to Westmont's natural beauty.

The campus consists of 110 acres of rolling woodland with a fresh stream running through it. The trees are mostly wild oak, willow, and western sycamore. The ground cover is multi-colored with sage, golden yarrow, California poppy and wild hyacinth. There are weekly sightings of gray foxes, coyotes and even a renegade bobcat who retreats after a brief glimpse, being shy of humans. On the banks of the stream, which is crossed by a rustic wooden bridge, one discovers in the early morning blue herons fishing, and black tailed deer coming to drink.

I met Ray early in the morning before breakfast. We both had come the day before. He recognized me from a documentary he had seen on the Irish Soldiers of Mexico, and I recognized him even at this advanced age of 82 from the unruly white hair and the square jaw. We stood together and watched the water flow under the bridge. "What a privilege," he said, "to be alive here this morning in a beautiful spot!"

"A blessing!" I observed

"Ah, yes," Bradbury replied. "An even more appropriate adjective for a Christian college. Do they call you Mike or Michael? " he asked.

"Mike is fine."

"Good, then call me Ray. Shall we head over for breakfast?"

We spoke about Mexico at first, testing the waters. He told me about his time there with a friend when he was a young man in 1945 and his love for that country. I had been teaching there for several years by that time and told him that I loved the country as well and admired the people. He asked if it was as dangerous as they said these days in the US newspapers. He observed that he was thinking of making another trip down there with Madeline, his wife, but that there were travel warnings in place from the consulate. I quoted the words of John Riley, "Be not misled by a country that has been at war with Mexico, there is no country as hospitable to strangers." He smiled in agreement.

"I don't do much reading these days because of my eyes but I did hear your audio book and enjoyed it. Do you know my work?"

"Yes, of course," I replied.

"What have you read?"

"Probably everything you've written, Ray, or close to it.

"Ah, a prodigy, after my own heart! And your favorite, or do you have one?

"Without a doubt, *Dandelion Wine*."

"Maybe, if you don't mind too much, you could do me a favor. Do you have a class today?"

"Yes," I said. "I am teaching a poetry session at ten this morning."

"Ah, so you're free this afternoon? Maybe you could help me with my class? It's at two o'clock. I want to do a session on writing short fiction and read a few excerpts from my work. But my eyes are especially bad today. I can do the talking fine, but it would be a tremendous help for me if you would read a few of the passages."

"I'd be honored."

To make a long story even longer, he dropped in on my morning session and sat quietly in the back. The session was quite full. I think a few of the students may have recognized him, but they didn't acknowledge his presence. He was quiet and unobtrusive. After the session we took a walk together around the campus, and then, suddenly, he apologized.

"I guess I didn't realize how dynamic a teacher you were. More like a preacher! Wow! You even had me going there for a while with that piece about the elevator crashing with the passengers on it. Goodness! And then the quiet piece about the boy watching the world go by and wishing he could be someplace else. So, I withdraw my offer. I'm very sorry, Mike."

"What? I don't understand."

"I'm sorry I asked you to be my reader. How misguided and arrogant! We should teach the next class *together*. I would love for you to read the passages from my books for me, if you are still willing. But I would also like us to co-teach and for you to take an active part in the session, read a couple of your things as well. Do you agree?"

The class

Ray began the class by introducing himself and saying a few words about his work. Then he introduced me as Dr. Michael Hogan, his co-teacher for the session and a historian and poet from Guadalajara. Then he turned the class over to me.

I began by reading one poem from each of us. The first piece was one of Ray's called "If Only We Had Taller Been" about the exploration of outer space. It was one of his more successful poems despite its formalist language and I knew it well, having heard him recite it on a tv program. In it he compared the spiritual outreach of America indigenous people with this generation's struggle to reach the stars. He performed it in November 1971. NASA's unmanned space probe *Mariner 9* had been launched earlier in the year and had just successfully reached Mars. To celebrate NASA's success, Bradbury and other famous faces (including Arthur C. Clark and Carl Sagan) were invited to convene at NASA's Jet Propulsion labs in Pasadena.

We ached and almost touched that stuff;
Our reach was never quite enough.
If only we had taller been
And touched God's cuff, His hem,
We would not have to go with them
Who've gone before,
Who, short as us, stood as they could stand
And hoped by stretching tall that they might keep their land....
Their home, their hearth, their flesh and soul.
But they, like us, were standing in a hole
...will a Race one day stand really tall
Across the Void, across the Universe and all

And measure out with rocket fire
At last, put Adam's finger forth
As on the Sistine Ceiling

And God's hand come down the other way
To measure man and find him Good
And Gift him with Forever's Day?
I work for that...

Then, I read a piece of my own called "How a Planet Stays in Orbit."

All morning the cottonwood
has been speaking. It began
when the house was barely awake,
not semaphore but a voice clearly distinguishable
which sang from all the nerve endings
which tumbled down the taproots,
which made the earth tremble
deep inside itself...

Here is the cottonwood, banal as a course in Early American Lit,

until one day when you could have been
anyplace else but were not
some poem sings from everywhere inside you.
Then the earth trembles.

It spins far out, twinkling toward Venus
like a northern star
A difficult line if we are
not quiet enough, amazed enough.

It sings:
This Earth is sweet as cherry brandy.
It rubs the warm Earth's belly.
And the planet spins in ecstasy,
it rushes out into space again and again
and then returns
hungry for our quiet songs.

One of the students, who was more of a literalist than a poet, raised a hand and said, "I thought that you were a science fiction writer, Mr. Bradbury. Your poem is more Christian fantasy than science fiction. The one by Dr. Hogan is also fantasy, I mean, what is the point?"

"Well, I really don't write science fiction. With the exception of *Fahrenheit 451. Martian Chronicles*, for example, is really fantasy not science fiction. Scientists tell us the *how* of things and science fiction spins off of that. I am more concerned with the *why* of things, especially as seen through the eyes of humans. That is the point.

"What is the point of having a universe with a trillion stars and a billion planets, including this Earth. Why are we here? That is a rhetorical question. It seems obvious to me that we are here to witness and to celebrate and pay back for the show. This is our work as poets and storytellers. We are here to be an audience for the marvelous. We have only one life, one chance to pay back for the wonders we've been given. Meanwhile, it is important that we clean up our act here on earth so that we are worthy of this gift. That is what the poem references.

"Is the universe really hungry for our quiet songs? Is the purpose to be reaching beyond our grasp? Yes, both those answers are correct. We need to keep searching, keep reaching out, but also to have a reason for doing it. Maybe to open more of the gifts, we've been given? As far as we know we are the only sentient and rational beings in this galaxy. So, this is part of our job. But also, to honor this planet and all its people."

Another student asked. "Do you both write every day?'

Ray replied, "Yes, I believe we both do. Michael?'

"I have found that keeping a journal is vital to my work whether I am writing history or poetry. It is not merely about events or encounters during the day, but scraps of conversation, images from nature, remnants of dreams, historical events. I write these down in a kind of shorthand and then refer to them later in the day to build upon them. Ray?"

"I usually find that just after I awake is a good time to write down all those thoughts and images which float through the mind when I am half awake and half in a dream state. After I do that, I have my coffee, make a bit for breakfast then return to my desk. I usually find that one of those images sets me up for several hours of writing.

"I like the analogy of the master violinist, Jascha Heifetz. He said, 'If I don't practice one day, I know it; two days, the critics know it; three days, the public knows it.'"

"How about the plot?" asked another student.

"I don't worry about the plot. That is one of the biggest hustles today. So-called experts writing books about how to plot a novel. Nonsense! I just find the image and the characters, and I find the plot reveals itself when the characters do what they are inclined to do. It is organic."

Next, I read a prose excerpt from Bradbury's novel where 12-year-old Douglas discovers that he is alive. He is wrestling with his brother, and they roll down a hill and he cuts his lip in the process.

"Knuckles struck his mouth. He tasted rusty warm blood...And everything, absolutely everything was there. The world, like a great iris of an even more gigantic eye which has just opened out to encompass everything, stared back at him.

'I'm *alive*, he thought. His fingers trembled, bright with blood like the bits of a strange flag now found and before unseen...'"

'I'm *really* alive!' he thought. 'I never knew it before, or if I did I don't remember...Think of it. Twelve years old and only now...Tom...does everyone in the world. know he's alive?'

'Sure. Heck, yes!'

'I sure hope they do', whispered Douglas, "I sure hope they know.'"
(from *Dandelion Wine*, 9-10)

The next piece was my poem entitled "Passing Through Virginia."
It was on the same theme but with a slightly different twist.

The boy balanced on the big root
watching the helicopter seeds of maples
spin like dying insects
is waiting for life to begin.
He doesn't suspect his green eyes
are more alive
than those speeding by him in cars.

It is difficult to learn
not to be waiting and thinking:
surely the best days of my life
are yet to be lived somewhere else
any place but this
is where love is and where
life will truly begin.

The crickets know nothing of such things.
Out behind the garage in the high grass
searching among the helicopter wrecks
of spun-out maple seeds
they sing lustily of this day
for the summer that is all their lifetime.

The discussion grew livelier as some of the participants related to the first boy and others to the second. Most came to the conclusion that it took a shock to realize that you were truly alive in the here and now. Most of the time you were thinking about regretting the past or planning the future. Or you were just getting through the day. His brother Tom knew intellectually that he was alive (as do we all) the group seem to agree, but we only realize it viscerally or emotionally on rare occasions.

Ray noted that this was the importance of literature. It took us out of ourselves, put us in the mind of someone else, say a 12-year-old boy, to remind us of what we have forgotten and what is truly important: the self-awareness of being fully alive on the planet.

Finally, we concluded the class with two pieces about old age. The first was again a prose piece from the lovely novel *Dandelion Wine* when the dying Colonel Freeleigh calls his old friend in Mexico City after the nurse leaves him alone in the room.

He asks the friend to open a window so that he can hear the sounds of the streets. The old man leans forward "gripping the receiver tight to his wrinkled ear that ached with the waiting for…

> *The sounds of Mexico City on a hot yellow noon rose through the open window into the waiting phone. He could see Jorge standing then holding the mouthpiece out, out into the bright day. He listened to the hooting of many horns, the calls of vendors selling red-purple bananas... He gave off a series of*

immense sniffs, as if to gain the odors of meats hung on iron
hooks in the sunshine...the smell of stone alleys wet with
morning rain. He could feel the sun burn his spiny-bearded
cheek, and he was twenty-five years old again, walking,
walking, looking, smiling, happy to be alive, very much alert,
drinking in color and smells." He died with a smile on his face.

The last reading was a poem of mine on a similar theme.

Those afternoons when the tendrils
of late blooming morning glories droop
against the whitewashed fence
and even the roses have lost the look of roses...
As if the planet stopped in its spin
and counterclockwise turned
and you are twelve again in a backyard
with the grass browned by the summer sun
while flies hover above a pitcher of warm lemonade.

It's too hot to play baseball and no one you like
is at home anyway: everyone's gone somewhere.
And your father's still alive in this memory
but won't be home till late
so you pick up a jackknife
and throw it at the side of the barn
and it bounces off, unbalanced:
another thing you'll never get right.

You know there's a time
beyond this when apples ripen in the fall
and the sound of the ball kicked in the air
and the crisp mornings, and evenings when
the harvest moon hangs so close it touches
the tops of the elms which canopy your street...

This time warp this
gibbous swelling of the earth that sets the rhythm awry
so that you feel every ripple of the leaves
and lean back against the grass and hear
the tremolo of insects and know that the world
is floating out over the edge of space
and nothing is more remote than your survival
or less imperative.   *(" And the Livin' Is Easy")*

"The past is not a *time*," Bradbury said after a short discussion. "The past is a *place*. And it's always there. Sometimes a poem or a passage from a story can awaken us to our own past and transport us there. Sometimes it can help us live life right now, right here. But also, at the end when you let go and drift off."

That was his gift to us at the end. He not only taught writing but living, and in the end, how to experience a good death, still vibrant and aware and present both there and here, more in love with the world for everyone we've met and everything we've experienced along the way.

CREDITS AND FURTHER READING

There are excerpts of poems in this book from various authors. In each case the title of the poem is cited, and the excerpt is presented as critical commentary or illustration of style. The transformative purpose of these quotes comes within the purview of "Fair Use" of Section 107 of the US Copyright Act of 1976. Readers interested in accessing the complete poems are directed to the book titles and publishing houses listed below.

Ai. "Woman to Man" from *Cruelty*. Copyright ©1973 by Ai. (New York, 1973: Houghton Mifflin).

Agha Shahid Ali. "Snow on the Desert" from *A Nostalgist's Map of America*. Copyright ©1991 by Agha Shahid Ali. (New York, 1992: W. W. Norton, Inc.).

Jimmy Santiago Baca. "I Am Offering You This Poem" and "As A Nino I Believed" are from *Immigrants in our Own Land and Selected Early Poems*. Copyright ©1990 by Jimmy Santiago Baca. (New York, 1990: New Directions Publishing Co.).

Ray Bradbury. "If Only We Had Taller Been" from *They Have Not Seen the Stars: Collected Poetry of Ray Bradbury*. Copyright ©1971 by Ray Bradbury. (New York: Stealth Press, 2020). Lines from *Dandelion Wine*. Copyright ©1957 by Ray Bradbury. (New York, 1985: Random

AUTHOR BIO

Michael Hogan is a historian, poet, teacher, and international consultant. He is also the author of thirty books, including a best-selling history of the Irish battalion in Mexico (*The Irish Soldiers of Mexico*) which formed the basis for an MGM movie starring Tom Berenger and two award-winning documentaries. His book on Lincoln (*Abraham Lincoln and Mexico*) is in over 800 schools and colleges in the US and abroad. His non-fiction books on Latin America and on teaching overseas, as well as his novels, have been best sellers both in paperback and on Kindle.

Dr. Hogan's work has appeared in many journals such as the *Paris Review*, the *Harvard Review*, *Political Affairs*, *History Ireland*, and the *Monthly Review*. He is the Latin American consultant to the State Department's Office of Overseas Schools. Dr. Hogan received his B.A. and MFA in Creative Writing from the University of Arizona. He holds a dual Ph.D. in Latin American Studies and International Relations from the University of Guadalajara and the Institute of Advanced Studies.

Dr. Hogan worked for three decades at the American School Foundation of Guadalajara as Humanities Chair and Advanced Placement (AP) teacher, and as a Humanities professor at the Autonomous University of Guadalajara. He founded the literary magazine *Sin Fronteras,* which has received twenty major awards for quality of writing and editing from the National Council of Teachers of English, including three times being chosen the best student magazine of all American Schools abroad. He has been a consultant to the College Board's AP program in Latin America and has presented workshops and keynote speeches at over sixty conferences in the United States, Canada, Austria, Poland, Malaysia, Mexico, Guatemala, Honduras, Nicaragua, Costa Rica, Panama, Colombia, Venezuela, Uruguay, Paraguay, Brazil and Argentina.

In addition to his work as an author and teacher, Dr. Hogan is a former consultant on institutional programs for the National Endowment for the Arts in the United States, a consultant for the Irish Embassy in Mexico, and on the land mine removal initiative in Nicaragua. His many awards include the Ben Franklin Award 2000, an NEA Creative Writing Fellowship, the Grace Stoddard Literary Fellowship, two Pushcart Prizes, the Robert Shafer Award for International Teaching, the DePaul University Celebrating Teaching Award, the Harvard University nomination for Excellence in Secondary Education, the medal of the Sociedad de Geografía y Estadísticas, and a citation for meritorious service from the Office of Overseas Schools, U.S. Department of State.

Home page: http://www.drmichaelhogan.com

OTHER WORKS BY MICHAEL HOGAN

History and historical fiction

Mexicans and Mexican Americans: Remarkable Lives, Unforgettable Stories, 2022

Women of the Irish Rising: A People's History, 2021

Guns Grit and Glory: How the US and Mexico Came Together to Defeat the Last Empire in the Americas, 2019

Abraham Lincoln and Mexico: A History of Courage, Intrigue and Unlikely Friendships, 2016

Abraham Lincoln y México: Un Relato de Valentía, Intriga y Amistades Improbables, Spanish Edition, 2016

The Irish Soldiers of Mexico, 2011

Los Soldados Irlandeses de México, Spanish Edition, 2012

Molly Malone and the San Patricios, 2011

Molly Malone Y Los San Patricios, Spanish Edition, 2012

Essays and other non-fiction

Living Is No Laughing Matter, A Primer on Existential Optimism, 2020

Newport: A Writer's Beginnings, 2012

Teaching from the Heart: Essays and Speeches on Teaching at American Schools in Latin America, 2011

Intelligent Mistakes, 2011

Twelve Habits of the Creative Mind, 2011

A Writer's Manual For Inmates in Correctional Institutions, 2011

Savage Capitalism and the Myth of Democracy, 2009

Mexican Mornings, 2006

Poetry

In the Time of the Jacarandas, 2015

Winter Solstice, 2012

Imperfect Geographies, 2011

Making Our Own Rules: New and Selected Poems, 1989

The broken face of summer: Poems, 1981

Rust, 1977

Risky Business, 1977

Soon it will be morning, 1976

Letters For My Son, 1975

Fiction

A Metaphorical Piano and Other Stories, 2013

A Lion at a Cocktail Party, 35th Anniversary Edition, 2013

A Death in Newport, 2011

www.ingramcontent.com/pod-product-compliance
Lightning Source LLC
Chambersburg PA
CBHW061611120626
46550CB00004B/1690